WRITERS AND THEIR WORK

ISOBEL ARMSTRONG
Consultant Editor

MARTIN AMIS

WW

MARTIN AMIS

Nick Bentley

First published in 2015 by Northcote House Publishers Ltd, Mary Tavy, Tavistock, Devon, PL19 9PY, United Kingdom.
Tel: +44 (0) 1822 810066 Fax: +44 (0) 1822 810034.

British Library Cataloguing-in-Publication Data
A catalogue record for this book is available from the British Library

ISBN 978-0-7463-1173-8 hardcover
ISBN 978-0-7463-1178-3 paperback

Typeset by PDQ Typesetting, Newcastle-under-Lyme
Printed and bound by CPI Group (UK) Ltd, Croydon, CR0 4YY

For Corrina

Contents

Acknowledgements

This book, although short, has taken a long time to write, mainly due to the fact that each time I thought it was close to being finished Amis would release another novel. Amis's prolific output is a cause for celebration but it can play havoc with a publisher's deadlines, and I am grateful for Brian Hulme's patient and skilful editorship, and all at Northcote House. I have had numerous conversations about Amis over the years with friends, colleagues and students, but I would particularly like to thank Fiona Becket, Fred Botting, Susan Brook, Peter Brooker, Anthony Carrigan, Jerome de Groot, Robert Duggan, Nick Hubble, Gavin Keulks, Tim Lustig, Scott McCracken, Martin McQuillan, Magdalena Mączyńska, Craig Melhof, Kaye Mitchell, Ceri Morgan, Jago Morrison, James Peacock, Roger Pooley, Sharon Ruston, Helen Stoddart, Joe Stretch, Barry Taylor and Philip Tew. I would also like to thank the late John Goode for first stimulating an academic interest in Amis's fiction. Thanks also to Katie Ryde for advice and corrections during the copyediting stage. Many thanks to Corrina Knight for her diligent and critical proofreading, and for engaging in discussions about Amis and other aspects of contemporary fiction.

I would also like to thank students at Keele University, Staffordshire University, and the Wedgwood Memorial College, who provided an excellent sounding board for ideas and discussion. I have given several papers over the years on Amis's fiction, but I would particularly like to thank Nick Hubble and Philip Tew at the Brunel Centre for Contemporary Writing for inviting me to speak at their research Seminar series; Tim Lustig and James Peacock for allowing me to give a paper at the 'Syndrome Syndrome Symposium' at Keele University in October 2009; Sian Adesiah and Rupert Hilditch for allowing me to present a paper on Amis at the 'What is Now: Twenty-First

Century Writing Conference' at Lincoln University in July 2010; and Philip Tew and Magdalena Mączyńska for inviting me to speak at the 'Satire Today' conference at Marymount Manhattan College, New York, in June 2008. Thanks also to *Critical Engagements* for allowing sections of my essay 'Satiromania: Postmodern Satire in Martin Amis's *Dead Babies*' to be redrafted for Chapter 2.

I am indebted to the Humanities Research Institute at Keele University for providing a period of research leave to write this book. I would also like to thank staff at the university libraries at Keele, Manchester, Birmingham, Staffordshire and the British Library for providing guidance and help on locating hard to find reviews and critical works.

Thanks as ever to my parents and family for their continued love and encouragement, and especially to Corrina who has provided the love, support and advice that made the book possible.

Biographical Outline

1949	Martin Louis Amis born to the novelist Kingsley Amis and Hilary Amis (neé Bardwell) in Oxford, 25 August. The family move to Swansea, south Wales, where his father takes up a post as English lecturer at the University of Wales.
1949–59	The Amises live in a number of locations in Britain and America including Swansea, Oxford, London and New Jersey, where Kingsley Amis takes up a Visiting Fellowship at Princeton University.
1961	Kingsley and Hilary Amis divorce; Martin lives at different times with his father in England and his mother in England and Spain.
1961–7	Attends several schools in Britain and America including Bishop Gore Grammar School in Swansea and Cambridgeshire High School for Boys; in 1965 he is expelled from Sir Walter St John's Grammar School, Battersea.
1965	Appears in the film *A High Wind in Jamaica*, directed by Alexander MacKenzie.
1967–8	Attends the 'crammer' Sussex Tutors in Brighton which helps him to pass the Oxford University entrance exam.
1968–71	Attends Exeter College, Oxford, where he studies English Literature and graduates with a First.
1973	*The Rachel Papers* published, which receives the Somerset Maugham Award, the same award his father received for his first novel *Lucky Jim* in 1963; works as an editorial assistant at the *Times Literary Supplement* and publishes reviews in the *New Statesman*; unknown to the family, his cousin Lucy Partington is abducted by the serial killer Frederick

	West.
1974	Has a brief affair with novelist Lamorna Seale that produces a daughter, Delilah.
1975	*Dead Babies* published; made Assistant Literary Editor at the *New Statesman*.
1977	Becomes the *New Statesman*'s Literary Editor.
1978	*Success* published.
1979	Resigns his post at the New Statesmen to become a full-time independent writer.
1981	*Other People: A Mystery* published.
1984	*Money: A Suicide Note* published; marries the American philosopher Antonia Phillips.
1985	First son, Louis, is born.
1986	*The Moronic Inferno and Other Visits to America* published; second son, Jacob, is born.
1987	*Einstein's Monsters* published.
1989	*London Fields* published.
1991	*Time's Arrow, or The Nature of the Offence* published and shortlisted for the Booker Prize.
1993	*Visiting Mrs Nabokov and Other Excursions* published.
1994	Leaves his literary agent Pat Kavanagh and moves to Andrew Wylie, who secures him a large advance on his next novel, *The Information*.
1995	*The Information* published; Kingsley Amis dies; learns that Lucy Partington was one of the victims of Frederick West; sets up home with the writer Isabel Fonseca in Primrose Hill, north London.
1996	Meets his daughter Delilah Seale for the first time. Amis and Antonia Phillips are divorced.
1997	*Night Train* published. His first daughter with Isabel Fonseca, Fernanda, is born.
1998	*Heavy Water and Other Stories* published; marries Isabel Fonseca.
1999	Second daughter with Isabel, Clio, is born.
2000	*Experience* published and receives the James Tait Memorial Prize; his sister Sally dies.
2001	*The War Against Cliché: Essays and Reviews 1971–2000* published.
2002	*Koba the Dread: Laughter and the Twenty Million* published.
2003	*Yellow Dog* published.

2004	Amis and family move to Uruguay.
2006	*House of Meetings* published. Amis and family move back from Uruguay to Primrose Hill.
2007	Appointed Professor of Creative Writing at Manchester University.
2008	*The Second Plane* published.
2010	*The Pregnant Widow* published.
2012	Amis and family move to Brooklyn, New York; *Lionel Asbo: State of England* published.

Abbreviations

Italics in textual quotations are all Amis's; ellipses are also his unless in square brackets.

DB	*Dead Babies* (London: Jonathan Cape, 1975)
E	*Experience* (London: Jonathan Cape, 2000)
EM	*Einstein's Monsters* (London: Jonathan Cape, 1987)
HM	*House of Meetings* (London: Jonathan Cape, 2006)
HW	*Heavy Water and Other Stories* (London: Jonathan Cape, 1998)
I	*The Information* (London: Flamingo, 1995)
ISI	*Invasion of the Space Invaders* (London: Hutchinson 1982)
KD	*Koba the Dread: Laughter and the Twenty Million* (London: Jonathan Cape, 2002)
LA	*Lionel Asbo: State of England* (London: Jonathan Cape, 2012)
LF	*London Fields* (London: Jonathan Cape, 1989)
M	*Money: A Suicide Note* (London: Jonathan Cape, 1984)
MI	*The Moronic Inferno and Other Visits to America* (London: Jonathan Cape, 1986)
NT	*Night Train* (London: Jonathan Cape, 1997)
OP	*Other People: A Mystery* (London: Jonathan Cape, 1981)
PW	*The Pregnant Widow* (London: Jonathan Cape, 2010)
RP	*The Rachel Papers* (London: Jonathan Cape, 1973)
S	*Success* (London: Jonathan Cape, 1978)
SP	*The Second Plane: September 11, 2001–2007* (London: Jonathan Cape, 2008)
TA	*Time's Arrow, or The Nature of the Offence* (London: Jonathan Cape, 1991)

VMN	*Visiting Mrs Nabokov and Other Excursions* (London: Jonathan Cape, 1993)
WAC	*The War Against Cliché: Essays and Reviews 1971–2000* (London: Jonathan Cape, 2001)
YD	*Yellow Dog* (London: Jonathan Cape, 2003)

Introduction

> 'The ideal reader, regards the writer's life as just an interesting extra' (*E* 117)

When Martin Amis produces a new novel a certain fizz of excitement circulates the literary establishment. The reviewers line up to either trounce or laud his new offering, and cultural commentators feel bound to offer judgements on the cultural politics of his latest book. This reputation has been built over forty years and he continues to be one the most important, well known and influential of contemporary novelists. His fiction has influenced a generation of writers, and many new novelists (especially young male writers) have often found themselves judged against the Amis standard. Amis himself has been influenced by dominant trends and thematic concerns in contemporary writing, and his novels engage with social, cultural and political changes with a satirical bite that is often as brilliant as it is frustrating. He has been associated with different literary modes throughout his career, in particular, postmodernism, state of the nation satire, pornography, parody, the mixing of high literary style with popular cultural forms, and even sentimentalism. In many ways a discussion of his fiction dovetails with the trajectory of British fiction over the last forty years generally, and a close look at his novels produces a yardstick with which to measure several key cultural debates and anxieties over the period.

He is also one of the most controversial of contemporary writers. From accusations of misogyny on the publication of *London Fields* in the 1980s, to Islamaphobia in some of his writings after 9/11, to more recent inflammatory comments on an ageing population, and patronizing representations of the British working class, Amis has continued to provoke and often offend in his fiction and cultural commentary. His style is purposely controversial and one of the legacies he has bequeathed to contemporary fiction is the interrogation of serious moral and ethical situations couched in a style of dark satirical comedy that appears at first to be wholly inappropriate. From the presentation of an over-cocky teenager in his first novel *The Rachel Papers*, to the opening of his most recent, *Lionel Asbo*, in which the reader is introduced on the first page to perhaps the only example in literary fiction of a grandmother–grandson sexual affair, his method could be said to stimulate controversy through exaggerations. There have also been the public spats with fellow writers and academics such as A. S. Byatt, Julian Barnes and Terry Eagleton, and celebrity figures such as Anna Ford and Katie Price. Through all this it is sometimes difficult to focus on what has remained the core of his writing: the novels.

Amis has a character in *The Information* say 'People are very interested in writers. Successful ones. More interested in the writers than the writing. In the writers' lives. For some reason' (*I* 131).[1] This has often been the case with Amis, and perhaps he has invited (whether consciously or not) public interest in his life as much as his work. This book attempts, however, as far as possible, to concentrate on the fiction, and to try to achieve that (now relatively old) new critical prescription of concentrating on the words on the page. That the fictional words inevitably intersect with the non-fiction (both from Amis and those writing about him) will be addressed where deemed relevant, but the novels themselves are the primary focus. A broadly chronological approach will be taken, although each chapter highlights a specific aspect of the chosen novels that connects with Amis's fiction generally. It will attempt to offer a critical appraisal and engagement with his work, identifying what I think are his literary qualities, but also identifying the limitations and sometimes frustrating aspects of his writing, especially in terms of its cultural politics. Given the kind of writer he is, these often overlap.

Since his first novel of 1972, Amis's fictional output has been fairly consistent, and with the exception of a few longer gaps between novels has roughly been about one every three years. This has been interspersed with other writing including some excellent critical essays, literary criticism and journalism, collected in the books *Invasion of the Space Invaders*, *The Moronic Inferno and Other Visits to America*, *Visiting Mrs Nabokov*, *The War Against Cliché* and *The Second Plane*; and several short stories that are collected in two volumes: *Einstein's Monsters* and *Heavy Water and Other Stories*.

Much of the discussion of the quality of his fiction lies in his stylistic control and prowess. The typical Amis paragraph offers the reader a biting observation of some contemporary cultural condition that can best be described as a high cultural treatment of low cultural subject matter, and it is this combination that drives much of the comedy – a comedy of inappropriate stylistic juxtapositions. This style in itself is provocative and can be accused of condescension: the patrician stylist offering an implicit judgemental tone on an intellectually inferior character. This is sometimes achieved through ironic distance in the first person narrations, sometimes through direct observation from an external narrator. However, it soon becomes apparent that the distance between the tone and the subject matter is much more problematic than it at first appears, and the attraction to the dark, seedy underworld (often exaggerated and exoticized) is engendered in author and reader alike. Throughout his career, however, Amis has emphasized the importance of the stylistic quality of his writing. He has often stated that for him, 'style is morality', and this conflation of the aesthetic and the moral is often at the root of the negative comments his fiction has drawn.[2] His writing beautifully expresses a morally ugly world. As Adam Mars-Jones writes: 'Amis doesn't so much inhabit his characters as leave them to seethe like charged rods in a viscous bath of language. The pleasures of reading Amis are electrolytic'.[3]

In a discussion with any reader of Amis, it will not be long before someone notes that either they don't like any of his characters, or that they are not realistic. These are valid criticisms, but they do not get us very far with an analysis of Amis's fiction. Firstly, he is not in the business of producing characters with which the reader will automatically sympathize, and indeed one of the distinctive features of his fiction is that he wants to examine the darker aspects of human nature through characters that challenge us directly. Often these aspects are the product of the societies through which the characters move and have been influenced. George Eliot's idea that the primary aim of fiction is to extend the reader's sympathies comes up against several hurdles in Amis's fiction, and there are many of his novels where none of the characters can be allowed much straightforward sympathy.[4] Amis's influences are Swift, Dostoevsky, Nabokov and Bellow, where the complexity of human behaviour extends beyond any clear (and naïve) delineation of good and bad, and indeed one of the aims of his fiction is to persuade the reader to confront such behaviour in terms that reflect back on the society to which the characters (and the reader) belong.

Secondly, the accusation that Amis's characters are not realistic goes to the heart of one of the paradoxes in his fiction. In many ways, the novels engage in a realistic assessment of contemporary (and some historical) societies, but the form in which this is approached is often through exaggeration and hyperbole. If Amis can be described as a realist writer, then the realism is much closer to Dickens than it is to Eliot. In *The Second Plane*, Amis suggests that commentators often misread his characters because they 'respond not to the novel, but to it's personnel' lamenting what he sees as the kind of reader that looks in fiction for realistic or believable characters they want to 'care about' (*SP* 18). Amis's fiction does not operate in this way. Characters are deployed as parts of the whole, and if we do not like them, we are not meant to. Amis's social commentary works, as the quotation suggests, at the level of the complete novel: it is a combination of the character's outlooks, behaviours, what is influencing them, and ultimately their fate that tells us about where our sympathies and judgements should lie.

It is in this context that we can begin to identify the qualities of Amis's fiction: his attempt to conjoin characters who have alternative or oppositional ways of thinking with established and residual moral and ethical frameworks. I argue in this book with respect to several novels that although Amis can in no way be described as a Marxist writer, many of the approaches he deploys for the analysis of contemporary political and ideological frameworks can be approached through models developed in Marxist literary and cultural criticism. In many ways Amis's fiction can be compared with Bertolt Brecht's model of epic theatre in which dramatic narratives should not exist in a kind of aesthetic vacuum, but actively point the audience's social conscience to the ideological and political contexts prevailing in the world outside the theatre. In many ways Amis's use of characters and plots do a similar thing in fiction. However, if Brecht's approach can be described as part of a modernist aesthetic with a clear political agenda, then Amis is closer to a postmodern approach in the sense that the cultural debates that his work engenders are far more politically fluid and contentious than Brecht's Marxism.

As with Brecht, the reader is encouraged to consider what happens when differing ethical systems and ideological outlooks collide. Often this is the juxtaposition of, to use Raymond Williams's useful terms in this context, dominant, residual and emerging discourses or ideologies.[5] Amis's fiction often stimulates by the shock of the new when it rubs up against the decline of the old, lingering in the midst of contemporary life as it is in the process of restructuring itself. This could potentially make him a conservative author, and the talk of cultural decline he often espouses supports this position. However, the point of view is often equivocal, making it unclear whether the fiction is satirical of the new society that is emerging, or of the outmoded ways in which some of his characters attempt to continue to apply redundant ethical judgements.

Much of his writing, therefore, is encapsulated in the contradictory nature of the term postmodernism. It is both of the present, but envisages a near future in which the parameters have changed. The characters he describes are often left floundering in the space between the established and the new, and it is the moral equivocations that inevitably arise in this in-between space that drive much of the comic and satirical force of the fiction. Amis has now been writing for over forty years and inevitably these cultural parameters have shifted in differing ways. In some of his novels he attempts to engage with the very modernity of the present, and indeed two of his novels, *Dead Babies* and *London Fields,* project ten years into the future to foreground the very *postness* of their postmodernity. Others, however, are historical in their return to moments in the twentieth century in which received moral and ethical codes have been suspended, most notably *Time's Arrow* and *The House of Meetings*; and in *The Pregnant Widow* to a point of transition in the established relationships between the sexes in the midst of the feminist and sexual revolutions of the 1960s and 1970s.

Despite responding to changing social and cultural mores, however, there have been a number of consistent subjects and themes to which he has returned. In an interview with Jonathan Heawood for the *Observer Review* in 2002, Amis reflects on his own work with reference to Graham Greene's in the following terms: 'You can say of Graham Greene that he wrote about the same things but he just got older as he did them. The perspective is like a shadow moving across a lawn'.[6] This has become increasingly appropriate to Amis's fiction as it has moved into the second decade of the twenty-first century. It continues to explore the recurring themes of interrogating Britain's complex and nuanced class system; the relationship between the genders; the nature of what he perceives as a long narrative of national decline in Britain; and the exploration of characters with whom the reader struggles to have sympathy, all approached in a writing style that locates its satirical wit in an abundance of well-crafted sentences.

1

Amis and Father: *The Rachel Papers* and *Experience*

> 'When you begin a novel at the age of twenty-one (or so I found), all you've got to go on is your own consciousness; autobiography is forced on you because there *isn't* anything else' (*E* 264)

THE RACHEL PAPERS (1973)

Martin Amis's first novel, *The Rachel Papers*, represents him setting out his stall as a novelist and is, in part, an announcement of a new kind of British fiction that distances itself from the writers of his father's generation. Furthermore, it establishes Amis's *oeuvre* in terms of its provocative engagement with issues of sexuality, class, and social and cultural politics more broadly. The central character of the novel, Charles Highway is a sex-obsessed teenager who vacillates from displaying a self-confident superiority towards all around him, to a feeling of loss of control reflected in the superficiality of the emotional relationships he has with family, friends and sexual partners. It has often been identified as an autobiographical novel, with Amis and Charles following a similar adolescent career path. It has, however, as with much of Amis's fiction, a first-person narrator with dubious reliability creating an ambiguity with respect to how far Charles's views correspond with his creator's; and indeed Amis challenges an early reviewer who conflated its author and main character.[1] The fact that Charles is a talented literature student allows Amis to produce a commentary on various literary precursors and thereby marks the novel as an attempt to position Amis's individual talent with regard to the novelistic tradition, and especially with regard to his father's work.

The novel details the transition of the young Charles from his teenage years into what he self-consciously recognizes to be the next stage of his life. It presents us with the character on the eve of his twentieth birthday looking back over the last three months of his life with the addition of earlier memories and experiences. The structure of the novel is important in establishing the relationship between the 'innocent' teenager and the more experienced narrator of his own previous life. In this way an ironic distance is established between the older Charles and the younger version. Although he is only three months older, the central experiences of this period – his first serious sexual relationship with the subject of the title, Rachel Noyes; his coming to terms with his relationship with his father; and him successfully passing the entrance exam to get into Oxford University mean that he does see himself as far more worldly wise by the time he reaches his twentieth birthday.

The novel is organized into twelve chapters that have two parallel time frames. One of these revolves around the last five hours of Charles's life as a teenager, with chapter headings taking us from 7 o'clock to midnight. The second time frame is the three months leading up to this moment and moves spatially as well as temporally from Oxford in chapter 1 to London for most of the rest of the book, with excursions to the Costa Brava and Brighton, and journeys back and forth between Oxford and London.

That *The Rachel Papers* (as James Diedrick has argued) is partly a statement of intent for the new novelist – the staking out an alternative position from the literature of the past – works on two distinct levels.[2] Firstly, it is identifying the ways in which some past literature has produced a false account of real-life experience. This is primarily part of an anti-romantic attitude to literature (and to life). However, as the novel tells us, we must not always agree with Charles's often pretentious pronouncements on the literature of the past. In this way, *The Rachel Papers* is interested in announcing the arrival of a new voice and a new generation in English literature – a bold attempt, but as we shall see Amis has never been afraid of making bold and often provocative statements in his fiction. Amis is, however, a special case in

English literature (with perhaps the exception of Evelyn and Auberon Waugh) in that the dialogue a new writer might have with his literary fathers is, in his case, quite literal. Kingsley Amis emerged in the early 1950s as a new voice that was eager to shake up the literary establishment, and who was associated (somewhat misleadingly) with the loose grouping of writers known as the 'Angry Young Men' during the period.[3] *The Rachel Papers* contains several references back to Kingsley's first novel, *Lucky Jim*, and there is a sense in which Martin is shaking off the association with his father by addressing similar themes in a way that marks out a difference.[4] One example is the way the novel addresses one of the famous attitudes expressed in *Lucky Jim*, that 'nice things are better than nasty ones'. Through Charles, Martin makes a wry allusion to this sentiment: 'Surely, nice things are dull, and nasty things are funny. The nastier a thing is, the funnier it gets' (*RP* 89). As noted earlier, the ironic distance from Charles is a central feature of the novel, but at this point we are persuaded that he and Amis are in agreement. Alongside this obvious reference, there are other less overt allusions. For example, in *Lucky Jim*, Jim Dixon makes a series of crank phone calls to the family home of his main rivals, the Welches, and in *The Rachel Papers* this is alluded to in Charles's phone calls to his father's residence during which he fails to speak. This latter phone call works thematically, therefore, on a number of levels that connect a fictional and autobiographical framework of the son's (stalled) address to his father.

These silent phone calls parallel the 'Letter to My Father' that Charles is struggling to compose throughout the novel in which he aims to set down all his resentments, but which is never delivered. In one sense, the novel itself becomes the letter to the father; however, what Charles discovers is that his resentments begin to disappear as he matures, as he gains experience of life, and as he moves through his first serious relationship. In this way Charles equates to Gordon Highway as Rachel does to Charles's mother. There is, of course, a Freudian aspect to this scenario, a theme that reappears in Amis's fiction: Charles's resentment of his father can be seen as a manifestation of the Oedipus narrative. According to Freud, as the male child grows up he needs to step into the role of the father in his relationships with women. There is no clear attraction between Charles and his mother as there is, say, in D. H. Lawrence's *Sons and Lovers*, but the Freudian narrative also suggests that the son begins to respect the father once the resentment is removed, and this is achieved in Charles's case by being able to associate with his father's position once he has experienced a mature sexual relationship.

In many ways the novel works in the paradox between the two conflicting attitudes to the father (and, by analogy, to adult society generally). One is a narrative of independence; of staking the claim of difference from his father's generation. In gaining this independence, however, the main character comes closer to the position of the father, as one who has already achieved a position of independence in the world. As Charles comes to realize towards the end of the novel:

> I think one of the dowdiest things about being young is the vague pressure you feel to be constantly subversive, to sneer at oldster evasions, to shun compromise, to seek the hard way out, etc., when really you know that idealism is worse than useless without example, and that you're no better. The teenager can normally detach his own behaviour from his views on the behaviour of others; but I had no moral energy left.' (*RP* 220)

By the end of the novel Charles is able to have a man-to-man chat with his father about their relative sexual relationships, an indication of the distance Charles has come on his road to maturity. Freud talks about the way in which the male child negotiates the Oedipal crisis by displacing sexual attachment to the mother onto other women, and thereby stepping into the role of the father, and it is in the somewhat neurotic attachment to Rachel that this process is dramatized in the novel, evidenced in the 'papers' he keeps on her. This is part of Charles's maturation and he arrives at the end of the novel with a new attitude towards sexual relationships, and a new respect towards his sexual partners. One of the demonstrations of his new maturity is the ironic attitude the older Charles has towards his younger self, and particularly to the immature sexual relationships he has with women before Rachel. The younger Charles seems to see sex as a kind of reward for the work put in to achieve it, as is evidenced in the references to persuading young women to have sex with him as a series of tests, which he approaches as he would revision for an examination. This attitude is carried over to his early attempts to woo Rachel by taking her to see an exhibition of William Blake paintings:

> I went along to the Tate, I need hardly say, on the Saturday before, decked out like a walking stationary department, also with a pocket edition of the poet's work and a well thumbed edition of the Thames and Hudson [. . .] Two hours later, over barley wines in a pub off the King's Road, I swotted up on some quotes and drafted a few speeches. (*RP* 76)

In his immature state sexual pleasure is largely one way, not established as a mutual relationship; for Charles, sex is about attaining gratification. His move to experience is understood in his coming to realize, at least partially, that his emotional life has been overly rationalized, and behind this lies an idea that engaging in sexual relationships involves acting out a role. As Charles says to his friend Geoffrey: 'Who ever acts naturally with a girl? Do you think you do? How much of the time isn't it loveable vague Mandied Geoffrey, or big-cock groover Geoffrey, or just plain old honest-to-goodness *Geoffrey*, who doesn't put on any acts or play any games?' (*RP* 78–9).

In this passage, Charles emphasizes that with girls the whole encounter is an elaborate performance – even 'acting naturally' is a form of theatre. But this play-acting is not only restricted to Charles's encounters with women – it is part of his whole relationship with others. For example, in his preparation for the entrance interview with an Oxford don he rehearses different persona in order to achieve the desired result:

> 17. Enter without glasses : put them on *a)* if don over 50, *b)* if don wearing glasses.
> 18. Jacket unbuttoned : if old turd, do up *middle* one on way in.
> 19. Hair over ears : if old turd, smooth behind ears on entry?
>
> A footnote referred me to *Accents 7*. There I read :
>
> Adapt slowly. If wildly out 'posh v. regional' cough at beginning of second sentence and say 'Sorry, I'm a bit nervous' in voice identical to don's. (*RP* 199)

There are two levels of irony at work here. On one level, it registers the crustiness of the kind of old don that Charles expects to meet, and even though this is largely a part of Amis's comedy it is achieved through the exploitation of a recognized stereotype.[5] However, the second level of irony is directed towards Charles himself who, through his adoption of a style that mimics the authority-figure he will encounter, believes that he will achieve his aim. As with his attempts to rehearse his date with Rachel in his meeting with her at the Blake exhibition, his attempts to control the interview experience through surreptitious planning also fails. Dr Knowd, the 'hippy' don he eventually meets, proves to be far shrewder than Charles expects and easily sees through Charles's performance.

Charles's self-dramatization in the search for an adult identity can therefore be seen in his expediential deployment of literature as a means to attaining sexual success. However, the novel ultimately shows us that his adolescent response to literature has been essentially false, as is revealed in the interview with Knowd. The youngish don spots Charles's lack of authentic engagement with the literary, and the fact that he cannot respond emotionally to literature parallels his immature relationships with women. For the naïve Charles then, life is a series of performances, and this is an early indicator of Amis's interest in ideas of postmodern identity. In this early novel, it is not a more extreme model of postmodernism, whereby people unconsciously float between different identities, rather, Charles is conscious of when he adopts a certain mask. However, this interest in the distance between an internal life and the way in which social encounters operate at the level of performance and theatricality is a theme to which Amis returns in many of his novels.

EXPERIENCE (2000)

An alternative title for *The Rachel Papers* might very well have been *Experience*, the title of the first of two autobiographical works Amis produces in the first decade of the twenty-first century. It is interesting, therefore, to discuss his first novel alongside his explorations into the genre of autobiography, even though this book does not appear until much later in his career. *Experience* is, of the two autobiographical pieces Amis produces, the one that most closely maps the events of his own life.[6] This is addressed formally by alternating actual letters and personal documents with the author's commentaries and digressions upon them in hindsight. He thereby eschews the conventional chronological approach to autobiography, but in doing so achieves a similar ironic distance between the older self and the younger that he fictionalizes in *The Rachel Papers*.[7] His father represents the main addressee in the work, but Amis also responds to various important and traumatic aspects of his life, most notably the extensive, well-publicized, and in Amis's account grotesquely comic dentistry that he underwent in the 1990s; and his relationship with his cousin Lucy Partington, who was abducted and murdered by the serial killer Frederick West.

In an interview, Amis has stated that when writing *Experience* he would allow himself some 'novelistic freedoms' and that the book is very much a 'memoir by a novelist'.[8] The book is certainly an unusual form of autobiography. For one thing it resists a linear structure, much in keeping with Amis's fiction. The book is divided into two parts, the first of which is titled 'Unawakened', the second 'The Main Events'. The first part is organized around a series of letters (that Amis stresses are authentic transcripts) written mostly during the period of his early adolescence, the first being dated 23 October 1967 (when he had just turned 18) and the last, autumn 1971. This provides a rough chronological order for the first part, but these are interspersed with anecdotes, digressions and details of close relationships with family, friends and colleagues (and some adversaries) that range over this period and earlier. The chapters in this part are organized around themes rather than chronology – the theme being suggested by something in the letter that heads each particular section. This unusual approach to autobiography maintains Amis's experimental approach to writing and, far from suffering from the lack of a chronologizing structure, makes the book a fascinating account of his life. As with all autobiography, Amis is selective with the aspects of his life he wants to write about, but he is clearly open about this selectivity, and this becomes part of the self-reflexive flavour of the book's approach to the genre. Despite the discussion of intimate and private relationships and experiences, there are places that he does not go, for example there is little detail of his divorce other than an account of the advice his father gave him on the matter.

The second part of the book details events that have had a particularly profound effect on Amis's life: the death of his father in 1995; the first meeting in 1996 with his daughter Delilah Seale when she was 19; and the birth of his two daughters, Fernanda and Clio, with his second wife Isabel Fonseca, in 1997 and 1999 respectively. It is significant that each of these events stresses the importance of family relationships for a writer who often appears in his fiction to be more suspicious and cynical of the ways in which family members relate to each other. Although part two reserves space for these 'main events', the relationship between Martin and his father Kingsley is a recurring subject throughout the book, and in many ways *Experience* represents a 'Letter to My Father' of the kind that Charles failed to deliver in *The Rachel Papers*. Like the letter in the novel, *Experience* is more of a cathartic experience than a communication to the living father, although, as in the novel, Amis is able to overcome in the later stages of Kingsley's final illness the differences they had. The novelist son addresses his novelist father by way of exploring the relationship with his own two sons Jacob and Louis, which forms a parallel and often a point of contrast to Kingsley's relationship with Martin and his elder brother Philip. Martin's sister, Sally, also appears in the book but less often than Philip.[9] Two of the other main themes of the book supply elements of (dark) comedy and horrific tragedy (although the word hardly seems sufficient given the circumstances). The first of these involves a detailed description of Amis's dentistry; the second a coming to terms with the discovery that his cousin Lucy Partington, who disappeared in 1973, was a victim of the serial killer, Frederick West.

The comedy is provided by Amis's account of his often-agonizing experiences with his teeth and the consequent visits to numerous dentists and specialists. That Amis should choose his teeth as a subject is partly to do with him 'setting the record straight' concerning the bad publicity he received around the time he was writing *The Information*. At this period, Amis was castigated in the press for ditching his long-term agent, Pat Kavanagh (who was married at the time to the author Julian Barnes, one of Amis's erstwhile friends) and moving to New York agent Andrew Wylie, nicknamed the Jackal, who was considered to be a much more aggressive negotiator.[10] The alleged advance that Amis received as a consequence of his move from the publishers Jonathan Cape to Harper Collins, provided extra fuel for the papers, who publicized Amis spending a large amount of this advance on cosmetic dentistry. A large part of *Experience* concerns Amis showing us in great and often comic detail that the dentistry he suffered was far from purely cosmetic. In fact Amis uses the teeth/dentist theme to explore wider issues with respect to moments of change in the life of the author. The descriptions he supplies of the traumatic moments he spends in 'the hands of Mike Szabatura', his dentist, allow Amis to explore the intimate relationship an individual has with a member of the medical profession that blurs the boundaries between close physical contact and a strictly financial relationship. One particularly significant moment in this narrative of dental reconstruction is the moment that he comes to terms with losing his top set of teeth, reflection on which provides him with a graphic image of his own mortality: 'My face seemed to me, not vacant (far from it), but strangely vacated. And when and if I opened my mouth before a mirror there was that void, that tunnel to oblivion. In addition, my eyes, I thought, showed the knowledge of that tunnel, and of what it meant' (*E* 152).

The 'new face' that Amis seems to have acquired also appears to change the relationship he has with those close to him, marking a brief and yet important moment of transition, for example in his relationship with his sons: 'The boys didn't look at me so much as watch me, their parody father. *That* father has gone; this father has come' (*E* 169). Although he later recognizes that the change was only temporary, Amis builds this experience into his broader narrative of significant moments that profoundly register the awareness of ageing. In typical Amis style, however, he is able to introduce a darkly comic attitude to these reflections on the transitory nature of existence. In one section he describes how going to buy his first tube of denture fixative reminds him of earlier embarrassing encounters in chemist shops:

> As I geared up for the job – indeed, as I circled a couple of plausible outlets – I realised that this business sharply reminded me of another business: buying condoms for the first time, thirty years ago [...] And it made me give a groan of defeated laughter. Because the

> earlier initiation was one of potent arrival, prefiguring insuperable treats, whereas the second – well, the second was all travesty, and pointed in the other direction with its mottled and rigid thumb. (*E* 161)

Here, Amis succeeds in defamiliarizing a stock subject for comedy: the shy adolescent attempting to buy condoms by associating it with intimations of mortality. In making this connection, the older, wiser Amis is able to mock the anxieties of youth, while at the same time being envious of the youthful condition that is a necessary prerequisite for the circumstances that produced those anxieties.

Another way in which the Amis of the present is able to look back on his youthful past is through the inclusion of past letters, which in the first part of the book all come from a period in his late adolescence and early adulthood. This important period shows Amis developing his philosophical attitudes and literary style. Thematically, the letters provide a vehicle that is similar to his first novel: the voice of critical maturity casting an ironic eye over a previous, and highly pretentious, version of the self. Amis identifies in particular an embarrassingly flamboyant style in his early letters and manner, so much so that he gives this younger manifestation of himself the title 'Osric' after the character with similar artistic pretensions in *Hamlet* (*E* 15, 107).

This theme of looking back on previous versions of the self is also developed through the relationship the book presents between states of innocence and experience, or more accurately the events and periods in which the former makes way for the latter. Much of this theme is related to the sections of the book that address his coming to terms with the facts surrounding the disappearance and death of Lucy Partington. Amis's account of this traumatic experience is an attempt to retrieve some solace from the terrible event by contrasting Lucy's intelligence and humanity with the cruelty and cowardice of her killer. In one poignant section, for example, he compares a letter West wrote while in prison, to one of Lucy's poems (*E* 172). Although he commendably resists the temptation to reduce this to a tabloid opposition of good and evil, he emphasizes the inherent goodness and courage in Lucy's character: 'Everything about her, even her name, pointed towards the light' (*E* 172). Much of this turns on the attempt by Amis to convince himself that

Lucy's strong character would ensure that she was able to stand up to West in such a way that her death would have been quick. This belief is partly based on the power and strength of Lucy's presence as he experienced it when they were children and young adults. Of course, we can never know the actual details of the events leading up to Lucy's death, but Amis's account provides a narrative emphasizing the victory of moral strength over the cowardice of the serial abuser and murderer.

The Lucy Partington narrative is also integral to the overall movement of the book as a transition from innocence to experience. As Amis remembers on the discovery of Lucy's disappearance: 'Over the Christmas of 1973, experience – in the form, as I now see it, of an acquaintance with infinite fear – entered my life and took up residence in my unconscious mind' (*E* 36). That the unconscious fuels the production of fiction, shows that for Amis, the control the author has over the stories and characters he creates is not straightforward, and fiction can, therefore, reveal hidden anxieties and fears from the unconscious mind. He suggests that the unconscious fear raised by Lucy's disappearance resurfaces in his novels after 1973, especially in his portrayal of the insomniac Mary in *Other People*, but also Ursula Riding in *Success* and Nicola Six in *London Fields*.

One of the other instances from early childhood that mark Amis's move from innocence to experience is his parents' separation and, in particular, the discovery that his father was having an affair. This knowledge was given to Amis, somewhat insensitively by a friend of the Partingtons, Eva Garcia, while he was holidaying with them in Wales. As Amis recognizes later: 'Only when I came to write the present book did I realise how much I lost and how far I fell in the course of that brief sentence: "You know your father...?"' (*E* 142). The significance of this traumatic discovery is only fully realized in Amis's later life, however, and the effect is represented in his overall structuring of the move towards experience. Amis evokes a deeper narrative structure by associating words such as 'fell', the 'garden' and 'innocence', all of which act as an analogy to the biblical fall of man. He also refers earlier, to the place where this experience takes place, St David's, as 'a geographical epiphany'. This is part of Amis's attempt to place greater significance on moments in one's life by attaching them to biblical or mythopoetic moments;

an aspect of the text that is borrowed from one of his main literary influences, James Joyce. In many ways *Experience* often reads like a *kunstlerroman,* the narrative of the early development of an artist or writer. Amis often refers to Joyce, although strangely he does not refer to Joyce's *A Portrait of the Artist as a Young Man,* a work of semi-autobiographical fiction that shares many of the thematic frameworks of *Experience* and also *The Rachel Papers*.

One of these themes is the nature of the relationship between a son and a father and, as with Joyce's *Ulysses,* the possibility of finding an alternative father. In the second part of *Experience,* the death of Kingsley becomes the main theme. As noted earlier, perhaps the most important aim of *Experience* is to readdress Amis's relationship with his father, and it is understandable, therefore, that Kingsley's death represents the main event towards which the book gravitates. Amis provides a moving description of the latter stages of Kingsley's life by presenting a series of incidents that show the deterioration of his father's health and faculties, a process Martin achieves by comparing the older Kingsley with recollections of his former self. In this way the account of Kingsley's death replicates structurally the relationship Martin establishes between his older self as the writer of the book we are reading and the younger self who takes part in the action. One moving example is the description of Kingsley's descent into speechlessness and inarticulacy as compared with his previous love of words; for example, the 'COMPLETELY RELAHIBLE' that he has written after one in a series of attempts to remember Martin's phone number. Another telling moment references the character Ronnie, who appears in one of his previous novels *I Want It Now,* and who is unable to say the sentence 'aren't all boulders old' after waking from a deep sleep. Amis reflects on this: 'Aren't old boulders all. Perhaps this is Kingsley's state: like waking from a tragic nap at a strange time of day. Ronnie is soon saying all boulders old. But what if you get stuck on old boulders all?' (*E* 319). This example poignantly foregrounds the tragic irony of the man who had such power of language and who has now declined into inarticulacy. Indeed, most of the examples Amis provides of his father's decline have a literary context or refer back to the life of Kingsley as a writer. Perhaps the most touching is the description of how the grand old man of English letters is reduced to typing the word 'Seagulls' repeatedly alongside numerous *i's* and *o's* (*E* 297). Kingsley's loss of cognitive faculties is also linked to the inability of Amis to respond to the situation, as he writes: 'We are an articulate family but we are heading towards speechlessness. We are doing what Kingsley is doing. We are becoming speechless' (*E* 302).

As with the Lucy Partington narrative, Amis tries to draw consolation from the experience of witnessing his father's decline and eventual death. He does this in one section by referring to the appearance of Kingsley in a dream: 'He said nothing (and I felt he didn't want to be touched). With gestures only, with looks, with pauses, he gave me to understand that I had all his trust – in the prosecution of his wishes, and in everything else' (*E* 363). Amis realizes that this is no supernatural encounter, but that it is a necessary part of the mourning process: 'A messenger from my own unconscious, naturally. But that's all right. Because my mind is his mind and the other way round' (*E* 363). The description of this experience also has something of the literary about it. It recalls the young Hamlet encountering the ghost of his father, a reference that, as I discuss in Chapter 6, resurfaces in the first novel Amis produces after the death of his father, *Yellow Dog*.

One interesting incident following Kingsley's death is the conversation Amis has with Saul Bellow in which the latter appears as a kind of surrogate father. Amis says to Bellow: 'You'll have to be my father now. It worked and still works. As long as you're alive I'll never feel entirely fatherless' (*E* 360). This picks up on a theme that runs throughout the text and relates back to *The Rachel Papers*. Formally, that novel represents Amis trying to find his own distinctive literary style in a world in which his father is already a powerful voice or, as Harold Bloom might put it, an attempt by a writer to follow through an Oedipal conflict with literary father figures.[11] Of course, in Amis's case it is literal. The way through this for Amis is not the rejection of a father figure entirely, but the search for a literary father whose work is sufficiently similar to his own to represent a development along a surrogate genealogical path. For all the social satire that makes Martin's and Kingsley's work generic cousins, the formal engagement with postmodernism and contemporary

American writing in much of the son's work distances him from his father's place in the tradition of English comic realism.

An important aim of the book is 'setting the record straight'. An irony here is that those used to reading Amis cannot completely detach themselves from the idea that narratives are not always reliable. In much of Amis's fiction the reader is persuaded to complete aspects of the story that remain unrevealed, and there is a similar effect in some sections of his autobiography. Amis is open to allowing that his unconscious may very well be at work in much of what he writes, and the blurring of fiction with memoir is in keeping with Amis's style generally; as we shall see in the following chapters, one of his main themes is the relationship between real life, the representation of real life in fiction, and the role authors (both himself and his fictional counterparts) play in this process. In *Experience*, Amis approaches this interest from the other end: real life accounts often read as if they are fictional. One of the reasons for this would appear to be that Amis slips into recognized fictional genres when writing about real life. So, for example, the accounts of his extreme dentistry often read like dark comedy, the description of Lucy Partington like Gothic tragedy; while the use of letters reminds us of the epistolary novel, and there is an underlying *Bildungsroman* element to his account of moving from adolescence to adulthood in the earlier sections of the book. That there is a mixture of genres is indicative of the complexity of attempting to write the multifarious experiences of an individual life over a period of several years. This fictionalizing approach to a real life works well in certain aspects, but produces a provocative moral jolt in the passages in which Amis attempts to come to terms with what happened to Lucy Partington in such a quasi-fictional form.[12] The book provides an interesting contrast with Richard Bradford's 2011 biography of Amis, which despite being based on several interviews with the author, has been criticized by Amis for being inaccurate in places, revealing perhaps something of the blurring of fiction and reality that lies at the heart of much of his writing.[13]

2

Class Acts: *Dead Babies* and *Success*

'Perhaps, like everything else, it's all a question of class' (*S* 45)

Many of Amis's novels are interested in the shifting dynamics of social class in the period from the 1970s onwards. This interest establishes itself early in his fiction. It is there in *The Rachel Papers*, but forms a central part of his next two novels, *Dead Babies* and *Success*. Each of these novels has characters from different social classes, and contrasts the upper-middle class and lower-middle class as well as characters drawn from working-class backgrounds, although his working-class characters tend to be one dimensional and are often based on exaggerations of popular stereotypes.

DEAD BABIES (1975)

James Diedrick, in his book *Understanding Martin Amis*, refers to Amis as 'a postmodern Jonathan Swift' adding, 'consistent with his scepticism toward totalising explanations and moral positions, however, Amis's irony is far less stable than Swift's'.[1] This reference to a sceptical attitude in Amis's work towards all totalizing theories indicates something of the postmodern form of satire that Amis employs in his fiction. In Amis's early novels in particular, the representation of a morally ambiguous universe delivered to the reader by an ambivalent narrative voice produces a radical form of satire that threatens to explode the genre completely. In several of the novels from *The Rachel Papers* in 1973 to *London Fields* in 1989, this satirical ambivalence in the narrative voice is formally represented in Amis's penchant for metafictional twists and turns that often serve to implicate the author (and by extension the implied reader) as a member of the group or attitude that is being satirized. This is produced, as Richard Todd has argued, by a series of doubles and doubling effects in these novels that often pairs characters with narrators and by implication with the author.[2] This kind of satire, where the grounding for the satirical attack is itself made unstable by the ambiguous positioning of the satirical voice represents a postmodern version of the genre, and it is in Amis's 1975 novel *Dead Babies* that this kind of postmodern satire on social class is most clearly identified.[3]

Dead Babies announces itself as an experiment in Menippean satire, an approach established by the quotation from Menippus with which Amis prefaces the novel: 'and so even when [the satirist] presents a vision of the future, his business is not prophecy, just as his subject is not tomorrow... it is today' (*DB* x).[4] Diedrick has noted that Amis's use of the Menippean form can be related to the publication of a 1973 translation of Mikhail Bakhtin's *Problems of Dostoevsky's Poetics*, which was reviewed by *The Times Literary Supplement* in 1974, when Amis was the fiction and poetry editor there.

Alongside Amis's correspondence with many of the characteristics of Bakhtin's typology, it is also likely, in his approach to Menippean satire, that he was influenced by Northrop Frye's definition of the genre in his *Anatomy of Criticism* as Amis attended lectures given by Frye at Oxford in the late 1960s. Frye suggests Menippean satires might be described more accurately as 'anatomies', especially in modern and contemporary versions of the genre, in the sense of a 'dissection or analysis [which] expresses very accurately the intellectualized approach of this form'.[5] *Dead Babies* does indeed apply itself to a close critical dissection or analysis of the body of British society in the period during which it was published. It is centred on the exploits and ideologies of post-hippy, post-countercultural youth, but in fact the targets of the satire are extrapolated to cover a wide range of philosophical positions circulating in 1970s Britain. These targets appear to include the post-hippy generation; upper and upper-middle class British youth (sub)culture; and the American countercultural movements of the late 1950s and

1960s. These targets are reflected in the title, and the phrase 'dead babies' is related to a number of contexts. For the American character Marvell Buzhardt, it refers to 'old' ways of thinking, those that he perceives belong to mainstream culture but are no longer relevant to the modern condition. In this sense, the post-hippy generation are 'dead babies' – they have the appearance of cool sophistication and intelligence, but are emotionally lifeless. The term also refers to the idea of loveless or meaningless sexual relationships; the term 'baby' being used here in the sense of a subcultural term of endearment for a sexual partner. This is the sense in which the character Celia refers to the phrase in her conversation with Andy about the demise of their relationship: 'Don't you think we must have made a mistake a long time ago to end up like this. That something went wrong and that's why we're all so dead now... Baby?' (*DB* 192). 'Dead babies' then refers to the death of love on a personal level, and as a marker of a culture's rejection of the idea of love through its concentration on sexuality. These meanings are added to the reference to the disillusion with the idealistic ambitions of the countercultural revolutions of the 1960s.

Although this rejection of the essentially American underground culture of the 1960s is the focus of the satire, it is clear that British (or perhaps more accurately English) society is the cultural landscape in which the satire operates. This is established in the main setting of the novel: the Appleseed rectory, a country house that represents a vision of lost Englishness. This environment has been invaded by a series of ultra-modern grotesques, all in their early-to-mid twenties: Giles Coldstream, with his neuroses about teeth and his mother, who is herself a representative of a declining aristocracy; Quentin Villiers, who initially appears as the ideal aristocrat, but who it transpires has been able to fashion himself in this role despite his uncertain background; Andy Adorno, a parvenu whose upbringing by Marxist parents has ironically produced a rapacious desire to grab all he can get; Diana and Celia, both of the upper-middle classes, the former disillusioned in her relationship with Andy, the latter about to be in hers with Quentin; and the repugnant, slapstick figure of Keith Whitehead, impossibly ugly and physically emblematic of the lower-middle classes, out of place in this cultural milieu. As the weekend proceeds, this cross-section of English society is joined by the countercultural Americans: Marvell Buzhardt, Roxeanne Smith and Skip Marshall, whose collective hedonistic pursuance of sexual and narcotic stimulation and experimentation symbolize a perceived Americanization of English culture. Each character then is representative of a particular aspect of contemporary English society in the mid-1970s, and together they are seen to be incongruous in such a setting as the Appleseed rectory. Each character also stands for a certain aspect of a debased contemporary culture: unrestrained excess and shifting identity, self-absorbed neuroses, an irresponsibility towards others, and a moral ambivalence. This juxtaposition of incongruities is signalled in the text typographically in a move to italics when describing the effect the contemporary residents have on the place: '*Appleseed rectory is a place of shifting outlines and imploded vacuums; it is a place of lagging time and false memory, a place of street sadness, night fatigue and cancelled sex*' (*DB* 33–4).

Signalled by the setting of the events twenty years into the future, one way to read the novel is as a dystopian warning. It is a vision of the direction in which England is heading and in this sense has a conservative agenda. The novel is set in the early 1990s, but as a form of futuristic social satire it is representative of a threat to the future of the nation if the social and cultural climate of the early 1970s were to be continued. However, the form of traditional, conservative Englishness represented by the Appleseed rectory is clearly not to be taken as a normative or advocated form of society on which the new cultural forces are threatening to impose themselves. It is true that the representation of a traditional English society *is* advocated in parts of the text by Quentin, who initially appears to carry some of the moral weight of the novel and who argues, for example, that, 'A hierarchical society is inversely reciprocal. The satisfactions of the higher echelons lie in command, protection, responsibility, in giving orders; the satisfaction of the lower echelons lie in docility, security, myopia, in obeying orders' (*DB* 175–6). As the text moves forward, however, Quentin is revealed as the psychopath 'Johnny' who has systematically targeted each of the main characters by leaving a variety of horrific messages and displays, which focus on their individual neuroses. Quentin's views, therefore, are seen, in hindsight, to be suspect. The attempt to regain a kind of a nostalgic rural idyll is also satirized. In one scene, for example, a picnic all the main characters have in a field adjoining the rectory descends into farce as they are forced to flee from an inquisitive heifer. In addition, The Tuckles, the aged, lower-middle-class residents of the rectory's lodge, are systematically victimized by Quentin and Andy in an attempt to move them from the estate, which clearly undercuts the ideal hierarchical society Quentin claims to advocate.

Consistent with certain kinds of characterization in Menippean satire, the characters in *Dead Babies* are based on a series of grotesques. Each character is exaggerated beyond a realistic description, a technique that foregrounds the aspects of contemporary character that is the target of Amis's satire. One of the most apparent grotesques is Keith Whitehead.[6] Amis's celebrated identification as a stylist is apparent in his characterization of Keith, where the comedy of the language exceeds any moral or sympathetic recognition of his human condition. Take, for example, the following description of him:

> The more clothes you took off him, the more traumatic the spectacle became [. . .] At school physical check-ups, doctors habitually refused to lay a finger on him, and the P.T. master threatened to hand in his notice should Keith ever set foot in his gymnasium again [. . .] Whitehead is, moreover, keenly appreciative of this state of affairs, well aware that by almost anyone's standards he would be better off dead. (*DB* 16–17).

This is comedy of the grotesque and reveals something of the carnivalesque spirit that Bakhtin identifies in the Menippean genre.[7] The reactions to Keith in the passage above are not meant to represent a realistic situation, but work through the unlikely reactions of those who encounter Keith. The physicality of this form of comedy reads at times like a textual equivalent of visual slapstick; the gross exaggerations are reminiscent of postcard humour, as in the description of the obese Whitehead family setting off on their trips to Brighton: 'as each toothpaste Whitehead squeezes into the Morris, the chassis drops two inches on its flattened tyres, and when Frank [Keith's father] himself gets in behind the wheel, the whole car seems to sink imploringly to its knees' (*DB* 163). The rather cartoonish way in which Keith is described here serves to emphasize the way in which the characters are dehumanized, an effect produced by the life-styles in which such examples of contemporary people exist. This comic approach to Keith also implicates the reader in the mockery that serves to qualify any moral grounding upon which satire conventionally turns. In mocking Keith's obesity and appearance, the reader is implicated in the stock response that Quentin and Andy (and most of the other characters) have towards him. Amis's text invites the reader to share the same amoral and judgemental position as the very characters it serves to satirize. If one traditional aspect of realistic fiction is to 'extend the sympathies', it would appear that in Amis's fiction that we are meant to extend the antipathies to individuals produced by contemporary culture.[8]

This approach to character reveals something of the complexities of the fictional mode (or perhaps more accurately modes) Amis deploys in the text. As with many of his novels, *Dead Babies* represents Amis engaging in a dialogue with traditional forms of fiction. In this case alongside the experiment into Menippean satire, Amis also offers a parodic dissection of the English country-house novel of the eighteenth, nineteenth and twentieth centuries. Parody is indeed one of the key postmodern characteristics of Amis's early writing. It is into the quasi-nostalgic setting of the country-house novel that the rapacious modernity of Amis's characters violently explodes in *Dead Babies*, opening up the form to an intertextual parodic reference to this tradition in the English novel. The breaking open of narrative form can also be identified in Amis's control of the structural organization of the text. Amis provides an organized framework to the novel, which contrasts with the nihilistic and hedonistic activities it contains. There are three parts, which represent the three days of the long weekend that represents the main time frame in the present of the novel: beginning on the Friday when the Americans arrive, reaching the hedonistic and drug-filled excesses of the Saturday evening, and culminating in the horrific come-down of the shorter Sunday section. Within this division into the three days, the 72 chapters are arranged into groups of ten (except that the first group has only nine chapters and the last group has only three). Each tenth chapter is titled with the name of one of the main characters and provides us with a brief account of their history. This structural framework serves to introduce the back stories of the main characters, who know each other because they are either all enrolled at, or attached to 'London University'. Alongside the main English characters and Quentin's American acquaintances, the only other characters who have any developed appearance are the Tuckles, the long-suffering residents of the Appleseed lodge, which is situated in the grounds of the main rectory, and who are victim to the ongoing attempts by Quentin and Andy to force them to leave.[9] This structural organization breaks down in Part Three of the book, as events get increasingly out of control.[10]

One of the main targets for satire in the book is the extension and perversion of the belief amongst some 1960s underground cultural philosophies that narcotics can offer a new and utopian way of encountering the world, the kind of approach that had been popularized by academics such as Timothy Leary.[11] Every member of the party at the rectory uses drugs excessively, and the American, Marvell, puts forward an argument for the use of narcotics in the development of a new way to understand the concept of humanity, through a radical philosophy of chemical and emotional engineering.[12] For Marvell, the human mind, and its connection with the body, is determined by chemical reactions. Being able to control those chemicals allows the possibility to control the mood swings and ultimately the happiness of every individual.

> *Fuck* all this dead babies above (*sic.* about?) love, understanding, compassion – use drugs to kind of cushion the consciousness, guide it, protect it, stimulate it [. . .] We have drugs to make you euphoric, sad, horny, violent, lucid, tender [. . .] We have chemical authority over the psyche – so let's use it, and have a *good* time. (*DB* 63)

In the figure of Marvell, the enlightenment project of using science to benefit man has gone awry, leaving a culture that consumes without any thought for individual or collective betterment. The pleasure principle has taken over for the Appleseeders, there is no restraint and they follow a culture of pure and instant gratification.[13] In the dystopian future of the novel, any radical political context for the use of drugs as part of an underground culture has been transformed into a purely hedonistic and morally irresponsible self-gratification.

Marvell's countercultural philosophy extends to his belief in what appears to be a completely free exploration of sexuality as pursued in his relationships with Skip and Roxeanne (and anyone else who might be willing). Events again, however, serve to challenge his utopian pronouncements. Towards the end of the novel Marvell and Skip rape Keith Whitehead, an event that undermines any kind of liberationary ideal that their open attitude to sexuality may have claimed. Nearly all of the other characters appear to adopt an ideology of free love, but again this is transferred from any radical potential it may have suggested in a 1960s countercultural context to one of selfish gratification with no respect or concern for the feelings of the sexual partner. In fact, as James Diedrick has noted: 'For all the compulsive talk of, and graphically rendered attempts at, sexual congress in the novel, only one couple consummates their desire, and this event leaves the woman in tears'.[14] 'Cancelled sex' in fact becomes one of the mottos of the novel. When Andy Adorno is eventually sexually aroused by watching a porn video that presents another example of cancelled sex, he decides to masturbate rather than have sex with another person, metaphorically revealing the onanistic culture to which he belongs.[15]

Andy is a child of the radical 1960s, the 'foster-child of a hundred post-natal waifs, the cosset of a dozen itinerant rhythm-guitarists, the darling of scores of provincial pushers, the minion of a thousand sick junkies' (*DB* 223). His name, of course, ironically refers to the influential radical theorist and Marxist philosopher, Theodor Adorno. As an ironic product of 1960s idealism and the child of a collective family Andy's adult life is marked by an overt promiscuity, and an inherent cruelty towards others. He describes himself as an 'ecstatic materialist' whose sole motivation is to 'grab what ever the fuck's going' (*DB* 175). He is, therefore, an ironic product of the 1960s radical, left-wing political agitators' dream of destroying the class system and its bourgeois family structures.

This target of the satire can also be seen in the parody of the alternative theatre that the Appleseeders go to see in London, the performance of which is invaded by characters simulating the violent, radical, agitprop group 'The Conceptualists'. This group is presented as purely terroristic, without any sense of a genuine political agenda, and which has resorted to mindless acts of violence as a kind of depthless simulacrum of rebellion. In its development in the 1960s agitprop theatre was, of course, motivated by an ideology of breaking open the class hierarchies in contemporary capitalist society. However, in this futuristic evolution of the movement (which seems to be an ironic reference to the Situationists) political objectives have been replaced by a desire for the nihilistic impact of a politics of shock. That some of the Appleseeders are attracted to this politically empty form of shock-performance is satirized in the way in which they have to barge their way through a group of tramps to get to the 'political' theatre.

> Twenty yards away, scattered about the dim foyer steps, a score of down-and-outs looked on fearfully as the Appleseeders poured from the cars and moved towards them [...] Andy raced on ahead to kick a gangway through the crowd – saying 'Get out of here' and 'Get some cash', occasionally boxing a protuberant head or stomping on a tardy hand. 'LEAVE HER ALONE YOU FUCKIN BUM!' bellowed Andy as a coughing hobo was slow to roll out of Diana's queenly path. Andy's heavy-duty boot eased his transit across the steps. (*DB* 113)

This disregard of the dispossessed is paralleled in Roxeanne's treatment of a homeless black man they later meet in a shelter. The attitude of the decadent upper-class Appleseeders to the London homeless shows the political emptiness of the so-called 'radical' theatre they consume in the face of the actual material conditions of the urban working class.

The implications of this lifestyle are re-visited on each of the main English characters at the rectory through the violent psychological attacks performed by the anonymous Johnny. Johnny sees to the heart of each of the characters' insecurities, playing on them by leaving signs and messages that provoke deep psychological as well as physical responses. For example, he targets Keith's collection of pornography as a way of revealing his anxieties about his lack of success with real women. Various candidates are put forward by each of the characters as to the identity of Johnny, most often the Americans, although Keith seems to be a likely candidate at one point, until he too becomes a victim. That Johnny is revealed to be Quentin is a surprise on one level, but not on another. Earlier in the novel, we have had intimation that Quentin's identity is based on a series of surfaces or performances behind which any sense of his 'real' identity remains hidden. In response to Marvell's offer to provide him with his desired drug experience Quentin answers:

> It occurs to me that one's mannerisms, one's behavioural ticks, are neither quite innate nor quite fortuitous. We project them as mechanisms of defence and appeal, of withdrawal and capitulation; they are means of stylising our attitude to others and to the world [...] I thought it might be interesting if I were shorn of these – my reflexes, my stock-responses – so as to become, as it were, socially unclothed. (*DB* 103)

Quentin's rhetorical flamboyance shows that he is a character well-versed in adopting roles. The irony that he wishes to be shorn of his 'reflexes' and 'stock-responses' is only fully realized at the end of the novel when these are adopted self-consciously as part of his role as Johnny. Quentin is revealed as the character that has been driving and controlling events throughout the novel, much in the way that an author might control characters. This association of Quentin with the author is a trick that Amis often uses in the early novels: in the detective Prince's relationship to Mary Lamb/Amy Hide in *Other People: A Mystery Story;* in the conflation of John Self and the character called Martin Amis in the chess game in the final sections of *Money: A Suicide Note;* and the relationship between Samson Young and Mark Asprey in *London Fields.*

It is useful at this point to refer to Bakhtin's understanding of the characteristics of Menippean satire, one of which is the presentation of alternative viewpoints offered in the form of a dialogue between characters. In number five in his typology of the Menippean form, Bakhtin states: 'Typical for the menippea is syncrisis (that is, juxtaposition) of [...] stripped-down "ultimate positions in the world"'.[16] In *Dead Babies* it is possible to identify such ultimate philosophical positions, for example Marvell's belief in the possibility of a psycho-pharmaceutical manipulation of human feeling replacing organic or spiritual human emotion is juxtaposed with what appears to be Quentin and Celia's belief in monogamous love as a true emotion. Similarly, Marvell's advocacy of a free bisexuality that cuts across conventional gender runs up against Andy Adorno's rigid heterosexuality. However, what makes *Dead Babies* exceed the Menippean convention, as Bakhtin identifies it, is that each position becomes unstable as the novel moves forward. Marvell's drugs, for example, evidently don't have the desired effect for any of the main characters and Quentin's avowal of true love is plainly seen to be one of his many posturings rather than the character being representative of that particular worldview.

As a result of these metafictional turns, the novel fails as a traditional satire, at least in the terms offered by Bakhtin and Frye, because it does not suggest a normative or alternative way of life against which the Appleseeders can be judged. None of the characters emerge as successful opponents to the dystopian lifestyle they pursue. Bakhtin defines the origins of Menippean satire as based on the carnivalesque and its hybrid function of the serio-comic; one which produces a serious judgement through mockery of the characters' comedic exploits. What you have in *Dead Babies,* however, is a form of empty or depthless satire. This can be seen in the off-hand and laconic description of 'those conversations' to the passages in which serious philosophical ideas are presented, which serves to undermine the seriousness with which the reader is meant to approach them.[17] What emerges, then, is not satire in its serio-comedic form but a pastiche or simulacrum of satire, with its traditional, serious function being undercut by the excesses of the grotesque characters and blackly comedic situations in which they find themselves. It could be argued that the trajectory of the characters' experiences tends away from the comic to the horrific, which perhaps produces an element of seriousness, but actually, what we are left with at the end of the novel is a series of personal, psychological neuroses against which any political or ideological certainty fails to establish itself as a convincing alternative.

Amis's fiction has, in this sense, become more serious as he has developed as a writer. His later satires from *Money: A Suicide Note* onwards have managed to combine a representation of the hedonistic and excessive behaviour advocated by many of his central characters with a critique of the societies that have produced them. With *Dead Babies* this is less straightforward and seems to be a product of disillusioned, early-1970s angst both with the old order and the failure of the promises of the counterculture to affect a serious alternative to that old order.

Bakhtin states with respect to the emergence of satire: 'It was formed in an epoch when national legend was already in decay, amid the destruction of those ethical norms that constituted the ancient idea of "seemliness" [...] in an epoch of intense struggle among numerous and heterogeneous religious and philosophical schools and movements'.[18] The same can be said of the 1970s, a period in Britain when traditional constructions of national identity had been loosened by the cultural 'revolutions' of the late 1950s and 1960s, including a broad democratization of society, shifts in gender relations and sexuality, and in the collapse of Empire. *Dead Babies* emerges in the flux of these heterogeneous positions or discourses and perhaps inevitably fails to find solace in any fixed ethical position.[19]

SUCCESS (1978)

Amis's third novel, *Success* continues to offer a satirical view of the British class system, but has a more narrow range of characters than *Dead Babies*, and although it includes examples of excessive behaviour is far more restrained than the previous novel. *Success* is tightly structured in two ways, firstly around the alternating narratives of Gregory Riding and Terry Service, brothers through adoption, but who are from very different backgrounds; and secondly, the division of the narrative into twelve chapters which take the months of the year as their headings. By this third novel it is becoming evident that Amis likes to give his fiction a tight structural framework on which he can hang the plot.[20]

Terry has had a particularly traumatic early childhood with a violent father, who, it is suggested has killed his mother, and has certainly abused and killed his younger sister. Through a mix-up with social services, Terry at the age of nine is mistakenly left to fend for himself in the family home for a whole week after his father had been arrested. When finally discovered by a newspaper reporter, Terry's story gains the attention of Henry Riding, an upper-middle-class philanthropist who adopts Terry, much to the chagrin of his son, Gregory. Gregory and Terry were born only one day apart and form a kind of surrogate twinship, while Gregory's sister, Ursula is the same age as Terry's lost sister, and these coincidences are part of Henry Riding's motivation for seeking to adopt Terry. This is the back story to the main chronology of the novel which is set when the two main characters are in their twenties. Due to Henry Riding's wishes, Terry is now living with Gregory in a flat in Bayswater, which, because it should have been Gregory's alone, contributes to their mutual antagonism.

Class conflict is certainly part of this antagonism, and Amis is clear to establish the way in which class distinctions extend beyond the economic into cultural behaviour, appearance and occupation. Terry works in a low-paid office job under the constant threat of dismissal due to the firm economizing, while Gregory has managed to secure a job as an agent for an art seller, due primarily to his accent and demeanour rather than to his intelligence. Amis satirizes the way in which the so-called meritocracy of contemporary British society is still largely oiled by older class prejudices. The focus on class can be located in the names Amis chooses for the characters.[21] Terry's surname 'Service' suggests his relatively lowly class position carrying suggestions of being 'in service' to the upper-middle class; whilst 'Riding' carries connotations of upper-class equestrian sports as well as a loftier position vis-à-vis Terry's class. In fact, the novel makes specific reference to the socio-cultural significance of names in a magazine questionnaire Terry fills in to identify his social status, where the name 'Terry', along with Norman and Keith, is identified as a working-class name, in contrast to the upper-middle class representative names of Sebastian, Clarence and Montague (*S* 58). Terry is acutely aware of his class background with respect to his adopted sibling, and the narrative suggests that this is part of his dislike of Gregory. Despite Terry claiming that he is now also 'posh' through his observation of the culture around him, it is made clear that this is not really the case.

In addition to personal names, Amis is also keen to show the way in which language generally is a cultural indicator of social class, in terms of vocabulary, syntax and style. As Terry notes, 'I know all there is to know about class. I say sofa, what?, pepper-and-salt, lavatory, vale*t*', and this indication is written onto the style of language given to both Terry and Gregory (*S* 58).

Compare for example these two descriptions of the same situation; firstly, from Terry's perspective:

> On account of the perverse design of the flat we live in (it's meant for someone flash living alone, or someone flash plus his girl), the trip to the kitchen takes me through Gregory's room, within a couple of feet of his bed [...] I am sincerely terrified of waking Gregory, despite my intense envy and disapproval of his freedom to rise as late as 9 or 9.30 [...] So I creep downstairs with a big mug of instant coffee and sit at my desk drinking it and smoking a lot of cigarettes (*S* 31);

and secondly, from Gregory's:

> Due, then to the perversely imperial design of my flat, the day begins with a quite traumatic glimpse of its second inhabitant, Terence Service. The blacking-factory he works for, do you see, requires him to be at his premises no later than 9 a.m., and Terry, a good simple lad, likes at least a quart of some cheap, piping beverage before trudging off. This brings him through my room and, invariably his cumbrous passage summons me from sleep. (*S* 40)

Terry's narrative is delivered in a language that is more everyday and colloquial: 'someone flash'; 'trip to the kitchen'; whilst Gregory's appears overly stylized and patrician in contrast: 'a good simple lad'; 'his cumbrous passage summons me from sleep'. What is interesting in this attention to style is that both first-person narratives address the reader as directly as part of what Stanley Fish has called the 'interpretive community' of a text. The division of language into class categories, therefore, extends beyond the page to identify the range of class distinctions in the readership itself. As with much of Amis's fiction, the reader is invited to consider and engage actively in contemporary cultural debates dramatized in the fiction. In *Success,* this is encouraged through the dialectics of language and class represented by the dual narrative structure.

This dual first-person narrative, however, as James Diedrick has noted, achieves much of the novel's dramatic tension through the relative unreliability of each of them. Diedrick argues that the reader is forced to fill in the gaps between Terry and Gregory's narratives as neither can be trusted. This is true, although I would further suggest that this balance develops as the novel moves forward. In the earlier sections of the narrative,

Gregory's overly haughty and condescending style tends to achieve a greater ironic distance than Terry's down-to-earth, if still partial narrative. Gregory's flamboyant style is gradually revealed to be an expedient way of hiding his real insecurities. These emerge more and more as the novel progresses resulting in the gradual building of empathy towards a character who initially appears to be an insensitive snob. In this novel, style becomes allied with artificiality and denial. Amis has commented on the idea that 'style is morality', but it is in Gregory's narrative that this is seen to be in a negative register: the more stylized the narrative, the less empathy is produced towards the character (*WAC* 467).[22] It is only when Gregory begins to reveal his true feelings (and, significantly, loses his protective and affected style) that the reader's empathy towards him begins to develop.

In Terry's case, the reader's empathy moves in the opposite direction. Initially, he is presented as a marginalized everyman who finds contemporary life recognizably difficult. Although clearly a 'masculine' voice, he appears as the stock of many a comic novel – the anxious anti-hero, a character whose anxieties stretch from his job, to his gradual decline in appearance, to the cessation of any sexual experience other than masturbation. The main context for this empathy comes from the traumatic experiences of his early childhood. Much of the effect of this experience remains hidden by Terry's direct address to the reader and it is not until the November chapter that he reveals the details of how his father murdered his sister.

One of the other gaps the reader needs to fill in relates to Ursula's narrative, and because the reader only ever gets to see Ursula through the perspectives of Terry and Gregory, her motivations remain unverifiable. Her experiences are only offered externally, so the reader has to imagine her emotional responses to her experiences with the two adopted brothers. An incest theme is presented in the revelations from each narrator of the other's deleterious effects on Ursula and their implication in her ultimate suicide. As Diedrick notes: 'Taken together, [Terry and Gregory's] monologues form an "X" whose intersection marks the death of Greg's sister Ursula'.[23] Diedrick goes on to highlight the way in which Amis identifies Narcissus as the guiding mythic principle behind Gregory's self-justification for initiating an incestuous relationship with his sister, suggesting that his self-love is projected onto Ursula. In this way his hatred for Terry can be seen as a way of displacing his repressed guilt onto a 'foster' double. Gregory denies to himself that Ursula is driven to suicide by her childhood experiences. Terry, however, is far from innocent in her suicide as he reactivates memories in Ursula by persuading her to replay sexual acts Gregory had forced on her as a child. Terry's motivation is revenge for Gregory sleeping with Terry's girlfriend Jan, not because he is attracted to her, but merely to antagonize his foster brother. As Diedrick notes, in this novel: 'The moral monstrosity spawned by [the] obsession with success is the central vehicle of Amis's social satire', and the homosocial narrative of class antagonism results in the women in the novel being the primary victims.[24]

So alongside the reversal of empathy between Terry and Gregory driving the narrative, and intimately connected to it, is an account of the changing response in contemporary Britain to issues of class. The novel in its state of the nation context is about the rise of the working and lower-middle classes as represented by Terry and the gradual decline of the upper-middle as represented by Gregory. The text is at pains to make this clear as we get to the closing chapters. Terry's narrative ends with him heading back to London by train, as 'the machine pounds along on slick silvery rails' associating him with modernity and the future, his last words suggesting 'I'm going to be all right' (*S* 223). Gregory in contrast is lost in the past and unable to escape his childhood experiences: 'I stand behind the row of birches. I'm cold – I want to shiver and sob. I look up [...] Oh, go *away*. Against the hell of sunset the branches bend and break. The wind will never cease to craze the frightening leaves' (*S* 224). The city-and-country division located in these two closing narratives suggests the relative shifts of power the novel has dramatized. That Terry is in the ascendancy, however, is paralleled by him becoming less likeable as a character, to the point where the reader may begin to forget his traumatic childhood. This culminates in the acts of arbitrary violence he executes on a hippy 'tramp' that he has an ongoing dialogue with throughout the novel. The implication here is of a Nietzschean will-to-power whereby the initially powerless figure subsequently gains power and decides to execute that power on those below him rather than fight for the powerless because of a shared understanding. Bleak satire of the human condition characterizes much of Amis's fiction and like *Dead Babies, Success* is keen to stress the unsavoury aspects of human (and especially masculine) behaviour. As in the former novel, no character emerges as a positive moral centre to the novel, revealing Amis's satire to be of the kind where no alternative moral framework is established from which to judge immoral behaviour.

3

Metafictional Mysteries: *Other People* and *Money*

'fiction is uncontrollable. You may feel you control it. You don't' (*E* 36)

Amis has often emphasized his keenness for focusing on issues of style in his writing. He stresses this at the level of the sentence and the paragraph, but it can also be identified in terms of his self-reflexive approach to the structure of his novels and the mode of narration by which he presents the story. As I have already discussed, Amis's fiction can be seen to be employing narrative techniques related to postmodernism and this is an important aspect of his fiction throughout the 1970s and 1980s. One of the most prominent techniques he uses in this context is metafiction, a form of writing that self-consciously alludes to its own status as fiction.[1] Amis's distinctive use of metafictional techniques interrogates the narrative contract between the author and the reader that is assumed in much 'conventional' realism.[2] This aspect of Amis's writing is also part of him establishing a distance from the previous generation of British novelists, a group which would, of course, include his father Kingsley.[3] The novels Amis produces in the 1980s are perhaps influenced more than his other work by metafictional techniques, and serve to establish Amis as a postmodern writer at a time when postmodernism was perceived as an exciting, and potentially radical, new style in literary fiction.[4] A theme that Amis develops in both *Other People: A Mystery* and *Money: A Suicide Note* is the idea of constructed and fictional characters at loose in the 'real' world. Amis is also influenced by (post-)Marxist theories in his use of metafiction, and both novels include characters, Mary Lamb and John Self in *Other People* and *Money* respectively, who behave in the ways they do because of their false consciousness and lack of awareness of the underlying (and often economic) factors determining their behaviour.[5]

Alongside a Marxist-influenced conception of the unreal in Amis's fiction at this period, there is a psychoanalytic context for the use of metafiction. Amis has commented that we should always trust our unconscious, and of course the Freudian model of psychoanalysis, whereby deeper unrevealed drives affect people's behaviour, lends itself well to the metafictional framework that Amis establishes in these two novels (and others including *Dead Babies* and *London Fields* in particular).[6] It is within these contexts of a post-Marxist understanding of ideology and a Freudian model of psychoanalysis that Amis presents the narratives of Mary Lamb and John Self. However, it should be emphasized that although each novel draws on both Marxist and psychoanalytical theories, their complexity means that they cannot be reduced to either system.

OTHER PEOPLE: A MYSTERY

Amis's 1981 novel *Other People: A Mystery* describes the experiences of Mary Lamb, a character who at the opening of the novel has completely lost her memory. This narrative scenario allows Amis to produce a picaresque journey of self-discovery, or rather an experimental approach to this kind of narrative in which the self to be discovered is a past self obscured by amnesia: a kind of self-*re*-discovery, as Mary Lamb tries to recollect and come to terms with her previous existence as Amy Hide. In embarking on this journey she meets characters from a range of social backgrounds and contexts, a framework that allows Amis to continue his social critique of contemporary Britain alongside the 'mystery' narrative associated with Mary's conscious and unconscious mind. These characters include Trev, a homeless and violent petty criminal; Alan and Russ, who work in a café where Mary finds a job; and Jamie, a rich bachelor who invites her to stay in his house and join several other women with whom he has had sexual relationships.

When Mary first awakes her amnesia is absolute.[7] She is unable to understand her environment, and the nature of the humanity she observes peopling it. This technique, as James

Diedrick has noted, shows Amis being influenced by the Martian poets, a group associated with the British poet Craig Raine working in Britain in the 1970s and early 1980s, and with whose work Amis was familiar due to his role as literary editor for the *New Statesman*.[8] This adult character, new born to the world, takes the name Mary Lamb from overhearing children recite the nursery rhyme 'Mary had a little lamb'. At a symbolic level, Amis emphasizes the innocence conveyed by this chosen name as it brings together the two central figures of innocence and purity in Christian mythology – Mary the virgin mother, and Jesus Christ, the Lamb of God. Her situation at the opening of the novel represents a form of resurrection, providing a symbolic context of a redeemed innocent dropped into a world of the fallen.[9] The adoption of religious allusion is ironic and Mary's innocence, as Richard Todd has noted, is far from benign in its effects on other characters. Her physical beauty and naïve character prove to be a lethal cocktail to those she meets, especially the male characters, and she leaves catastrophe in her wake by exacerbating to the point of crisis the anxieties that these characters are already carrying.

Mary gradually begins to construct her identity within the world through these encounters, and she also begins to piece together her pre-existence as Amy Hide before her loss of memory, a character that she begins to learn has manipulated others, been involved in some unspecified transgressions, and who is believed to have been murdered. Tracking her progress is Mr Prince, who is variously described (and describes himself) as a policeman and a murderer. On one level, *Other People*, like Amis's later novel *London Fields*, is a postmodern parody of popular genre fiction, in particular the murder mystery and detective novel. Prince can be seen as a paradoxical amalgam of the typical essential roles in such texts: the murderer, and the cop trying to uncover the murder. Amis also introduces a further characteristic to Prince, that of the controlling authorial voice and manipulator of characters, motive and plot.

Other People is the first of Amis's novels to have a female character as the central consciousness and focalizer.[10] Diedrick has argued that the novel represents a reading of gender politics as culturally defined. He is right to a certain extent, but women are presented in a contradictory way in which gendered power relationships are partly related to societal forces, but partly a result of what appears to be an essentializing view of gender. Although Mary is unconscious of the mechanics of sexual relationships, her encounter with Trev in Chapter 4 is tantamount to rape: 'Mary couldn't believe that she had done this before: she knew she never wanted to do it again [She] didn't stir for some time. I'm dead she thought. He's killed me. Why? How did he dare? And soon he's going to kill me again' (*OP* 42–3). Mary reacts to Trev's violence reciprocally by hitting him with a brick, and sex is thus initially established for Mary as an act of violence. It is only through her subsequent relationships with Alan and Jamie, and eventually Prince, that she recovers from this view. Mary's resistance in her relationship with Trev can, therefore, be seen as an indication of her rejection of the apparently naturalized inequalities in power between men and women in the society in which she finds herself. When Mary moves to the Church Army Hostel for Young Women, she encounters several women who have been the victim of male aggression and this aspect of contemporary culture is defamiliarized through Mary's perspective: 'Some girls kept having fights with their men, and always losing. They bore the marks. Why would a man fight a woman? Wondered Mary. He would always win; he wasn't fighting – he was just doing harm, doing damage' (*OP* 69). Later in the text, however, the power relationships between men and women become more complicated, especially between Jamie and the three women who live in his house: Lily, Jo and Augusta. Although they have individually achieved their own conditions of power, they reveal the ways in which sexual politics operates at emotional and intellectual levels, rather than the crude violence displayed in Mary's brief relationship with Trev.

The reading of gender as cultural also extends to what appear to Mary to be the bizarre codes of clothing that distinguish men and women. In an earlier section she describes the high-heeled shoes that she seems forced to wear as 'heavy curved extensions', concluding that, 'The idea was obviously to make movement very difficult, if not actually impossible' (*OP* 14). She eventually discards these shoes ('She bent down to examine them and found, to her pleased surprise, that she could remove them without much difficulty' (*OP* 15)), which is a small indication of her resistance to the cultural absurdities to which women seem to her to be subjected. However, her personal rebellion against the gendered cultural codes is not acceptable to other people and she is forced to conform by rejoining society's conventions: 'They stared; they stared at her feet; they had all grown used to their own devices [...] no one was intended to be without them, and she was sorry. But she moved, and kept on moving, because that's what everyone was required to do' (*OP* 16).

Despite these gestures towards interrogating accepted codes of behaviour, the novel oscillates between a cultural and essentialized view of gender. As this is presented through Mary's perspective, the essentializing view is often given the validity of Mary's defamiliarizing innocence: 'Women of this age [over forty] looked like men: they had given up the ghosts of their femininity. Perhaps life was just extra hard on women, or perhaps being a man was the more natural state, to which all women were obliged to revert in the end, despite all their struggles' (*OP* 86). Here, the rhetorical device of putting the cultural view of gender before the essentialist tends to favour the latter. Further on in the text, Mary makes observations about women's attempts to resist patriarchy by taking on characteristics that have been traditionally seen as masculine, a view that seems to be borrowed from a sexual politics reminiscent of D. H. Lawrence (a recurring influence for Amis): 'How shameful, really, that when women tried to be free of men and strong in themselves, they just watched the way men were strong and copied that' (*OP* 165).[11] As the novel was published in 1981, the figure of Margaret Thatcher seems to be looming behind this statement; nevertheless, it dismisses an important feature of second-wave feminism, and the point Mary makes in this context – 'Oh man... *Women* are the other people, yes we are' (*OP* 175) – is ambiguous in terms of sexual politics. This can be read both as an endorsement of Simone de Beauvoir's observation of the inequalities of patriarchal society, but equally as an invocation of the romantic inscrutability of women in much male-oriented discourse.[12]

Power, indeed, is a crucial element of the novel, and one of the targets of Amis's satire. He is interested in challenging the human desire for power, and it is in part Mary's understanding of the power that she can have over others that reveals Amis's bleak critique of human nature. The recognition that to become socialized is to be aware of the way in which individuals survive by manipulating others is part of the novel's trajectory from innocence to experience, and it is made clear that Mary has entered her final stage of recognition in the relationship with Jamie when she is aware that she can gain his sexual attention by feigning sadness. As in *Success*, power tends to come in the form of a Nietzschean will-to-power, rather than an emancipatory empowerment for a character that is initially powerless.[13] It is this element of the novel that sits uneasily with Amis's critique of some of the specific instances of power. Although, as I argue with respect to *Money*, there is a Marxist influence to Amis's understanding of the way in which money operates in contemporary British society, his description of power relationships in localized situations tends to follow a Foucauldian model.[14] In all the mini-societies in which Mary finds herself, a complex and stratified power struggle is in operation between individuals, sometimes based on physical violence as in the sections with the tramps, sometimes more psychological as with the relationship between Alan and Russ, and in the collective alternative family in Jamie's house.

One of the contexts for defamiliarization, which the novel develops, can be related to a psychological understanding of the term. In his essay 'The Uncanny', Sigmund Freud describes the feeling of *unheimlich* or 'unhomeliness' a person may experience when an object or situation simultaneously carries familiar and unfamiliar aspects, and according to Freud is a manifestation of past hidden traumas that have been pushed into the unconscious, or engendered at moments of transition in the psyche. Amis utilizes Mary's amnesiac situation to develop this sense of the uncanny, both in terms of her partial recognition of a previous self, and in the situation of characters seemingly recognizing her, but in doing so being shocked by a memory of the past. The psychoanalytic context of Mary's situation can also be seen in the use of mirrors and doubling in the novel, as Richard Todd has shown.[15] Todd's analysis steers clear of a psychoanalytic reading, but there is certainly enough reference in the novel to suggest that it operates with respect to models of behaviour that chime with Freud, and particularly with the strand of psychoanalysis developed by Jacques Lacan. The use of mirrors is particularly interesting in this context and suggests that Amis is cultivating the theoretical perspective suggested by Lacan's identification of the 'mirror stage' as a crucial aspect of the development of identity.[16] The novel can be read as a dramatization of Mary going through an adult version of this stage of psychological development, as evidenced in the various unsettling half recognitions she has of aspects of her former identity when looking in a mirror: 'It was Mary. But it was *older* than Mary. The face looked out at her defiantly, with perhaps the beginnings of a sneer or a snicker in the raised left-hand side of the mouth' (*OP* 73). At one stage the novel speculates that Mary's double-identity is part of the general human condition, thus extending the particularity of Mary's unusual situation to a general aspect of our psychology, as she observes: 'Perhaps every girl was really two girls [. . .] As she turned away from the mirror she saw the ghost of a smile from the knowing genius that lived behind the glass' (*OP* 75). Mirrors are present at significant moments of transition, for example when Mary finally recovers her lost identity as Amy at the end of the second part of the novel. At this moment she achieves maturity; and her descent into the fallen world is complete: 'The instant she threw the switch a face reared out of the glass, in exultation, in relief, in terror. She had done it. She had torn through the glass and come back from the other side. She had found her again. She was herself at last' (*OP* 185).

Dreams are, of course, another important aspect in psychoanalytic theory, and Amis also uses these as a way for Mary to unlock her past. As Prince notes: 'You know, don't you, that your forgotten wrongs will never cease to caffeinate your thoughts? [. . .] In the end the past will always be there' (*OP* 76). Mary initially defamiliarizes the experience of dreaming: 'She felt that dreams came from the past. She had never seen a red beach bubbled with sandpools under a furious and unstable sun. She had never felt a sensation of speed so intense that her nose could remember the tang of smouldering air. And the dreams always ended by mangling her' (*OP* 58). Dreaming both reveals the past, and represents the subconscious displacement of anxieties for Mary. In fact this dream contains a proleptic projection to the experience of the death Mary/Amy undergoes at the hands of Prince at the end of the novel as can be seen in the repeated line: 'She saw a red beach bubbled with sandpools under a furious and unstable sun' (*OP* 206). It is significant then, that at the moment of death, we have a return to a memory that Mary had in a dream, which is itself an unformed memory coming from Amy. In a sense, Amy represents the repressed unconsciousness to Mary's conscious ego, and the focus on repetition here gestures towards the idea in Freudian psychoanalysis of the repeated return of repressed memories.[17]

This psychoanalytic context also forms a significant part of Amis's following novel, *Money: A Suicide Note.*

MONEY: A SUICIDE NOTE

This 1984 novel is seen by many as Amis's most important; the text in which he most successfully balances his social and cultural critique of contemporary Britain, with an intensity and quality of writing, and an interrogation of the nature of literary fiction.[18] The novel has been seen as the quintessential evocation of the greed and individualism that marked certain aspects of the 1980s.[19] In fact, it carries over many of the themes he established in *Other People*, including his use of metafictional techniques, his focus on the foibles and misanthropic drives of humanity, and the deployment of psychological models drawn from Freud.

One of the most distinctive features of the text is the creation of its central character and voice – John Self. Self is the epitome of the greed and, as his name suggests, self-centredness of certain aspects of 1980s British and American society. He has a working-class background, and at the opening of the novel, has achieved a certain amount of success by working as a film maker and producer, mostly in the field of advertising. He is presented as an Everyman of the 1980s, or as Fred Botting has called him, an 'every-Self of contemporary culture'.[20] He is a kind of extended adolescent, still pursuing immature drives and entertainments although he is in his mid-thirties, making this novel a parody of the traditional *Bildungsroman*.[21] He is aware of his excessive lifestyle and the detrimental effect it is having on his body and mind, but he appears locked into a cycle of deleterious self-gratification, and, as he recognizes, his addictive personality is fuelled by the culture in which he is placed – 'I am addicted to the twentieth century' (*M* 91). As with *Other People* the plot is picaresque and follows Self's attempts to produce a film based on his own background and experiences. It sees him encountering a number of characters related to the film industry in London and New York, interspersed with scenes concerning his personal relationships with Selina Street, his girlfriend when the novel opens; and Martina Twain, the woman with whom he has a brief affair; and several returns to the 'Shakespeare', the pub owned by Barry (who Self believes at the outset of the novel to be his father).

The success of the novel lies in the darkly comic intensities of Self's first-person narrative, through which we gain first-hand access to his 'private culture' (*M* 123). It is apparent, however, that Self's lifestyle is expressive of the worst aspects of contemporary culture, presented in the novel as hyper-accelerated, onanistic and lacking human connection:

> I realize when I can bear to think about it, that all my hobbies are pornographic in tendency. The element of lone gratification is bluntly stressed. Fast food, sex shows, space games, slot machines, video nasties, nude mags, drink, pubs, fighting, television, handjobs. I've got a hunch about these handjobs, or about their exhausting frequency. I need that human touch. There's no human here so I do it to myself. At least the handjobs are free, complimentary, with no cash attaching. (*M* 67)

This passage lists aspects of a debased contemporary culture that are anti-humanistic, emphasized by the line 'There's no human here', in the sense that all human feeling has been removed from his cultural lifestyle. He is, however, aware of his predicament: 'It really isn't very nice in here. And that is why I long to burst out of the world of money and into – into what? [...] Tell me please. I'll never make it by myself. I just don't know the way' (*M* 123). Self knows the damage his lifestyle wreaks on his physical well being and he aims to offset this by gaining enough wealth to pay for a number of cosmetic and medical operations, showing how the bodily and the pecuniary are welded together in this culture. This focus is part of the general dehumanizing drift of the novel and Self often describes himself and others in terms of the animalistic, technological or post-human: 'I feel prosthetic. I am robot, I am android, I am cyborg, I am skinjob' (*M* 329).

The critique of the dehumanizing aspects of contemporary consumerist culture extends to Self's relationships with several female characters in the novel. His attitude to women is clearly presented as reprehensible and, as he recognizes, is essentially pornographic. This is most clearly seen in the relationship he has with his girlfriend Selina Street. It is clear that this relationship is mutually exploitative and based primarily on money, consequently there is no love or trust between them:

> I don't think Selina Street *is* fucking Alec Llewellyn. Why? Because he hasn't got any money. I have. Come on why do you reckon Selina has soldiered it out with me? For my pot belly, my bad rug, my personality? [...] When I make all this money I'm going to make, my position will be even stronger. Then I can kick Selina out and get someone even better. (*M* 24)

In a novel in which doubles are again important, Selina can be seen as the female mirror-image of Self, and as the quotation above indicates, *Money* presents a post-romantic world in which sexual relationships appear to be based exclusively on exchange value. Clearly, Self's attitudes to women are satirized, however the sexual politics of the novel is more complicated than the reader automatically rejecting Self's misogynistic attitudes because they are presented in such an excessive form. One of the most controversial scenes in the novel sees Self attempting to rape Selina. He is unsuccessful as Selina matches his levels of aggression; however, the comic tone in which the scene is recounted makes for difficult reading and removes any sympathy that the reader may have accrued for Self.[22]

This section of the novel alerts us to a central problem in the mode of narration Amis adopts: the unconvincing disparity between the nature of the man that Self appears to be and the powers of articulation he clearly has to convey his experience. As Diedrick has identified, *Money* employs the critical technique of the Russian skaz tradition as exemplified in Dostoevsky's *Notes from Underground,* in which an alienated narrator offers a perceptive critique of his society, from the point of view of a character whose moral outlook, or social class and education is likely to be a great distance from the shared projected outlook of the author and the implied reader, or a character whose social class and education is meant to be at a similar distance.[23] Amis's exuberant and stylized language, however, sits uneasily with the character John Self, producing a narrative in which the unattractive aspects of the central character are presented in a style we are meant to admire. This presents one of the main ethical problems that some reviewers and critics have identified in the novel – the difficulty of distinguishing between those parts of the text that are meant to show the excessive and reprehensible aspects of John Self, and those that are closer to a world-view supported by the author (and with which the reader is invited to agree). This ethical dilemma, however, is clearly at the heart of Amis's ambition in the novel. Self is a complex character that has a rich and often contradictory attitude to contemporary existence, and in that sense represents a kind of realism that eschews a straightforward opposition of commendable and reprehensible characters in fiction.[24]

The ambiguities of the novel's engagement with sexual politics, also extend to the way in which the political critique and the reading of contemporary economics are meant to be approached. For example, the following passage seems to offer a reasonable reading of contemporary British society in a voice that appears to convey the author's views rather than (or as well as) Self's:

> I came of age in the Sixties, when there were chances, when it was all there waiting. Now they seep out of school – to what? To nothing, to fuck-all. The young (you can see it in their faces), the stegosaurus-rugged no-hopers, the parrot-crested blankies – they've come up with an appropriate response to all this, which is: nothing. Which is nothing, which is fuck-all. The dole-queue starts at the exit to the playground. Riots are their rumpus-room, sombre London their jungle-gym. Life is hoarded elsewhere by others. Money is so near you can touch it, but it is all on the other side – you can only press your face up against the glass. In my day, if you wanted, you could just drop out. You can't drop out any more. Money has seen to that. There's nowhere to go. You cannot hide out from money. You just cannot hide out from money anymore. And so sometimes, when the nights are hot, they smash and grab. (*M* 153)[25]

The novel is set in 1981, when a series of inner city riots flared up across Britain. These riots were dubbed 'race riots' in the popular press as many of the rioters came from Black and Asian backgrounds.[26] Through Self's voice, however, Amis offers an economic reading of the riots, indicative not of the racial make-up of Britain during the period, but the effect of economic policies on those disenfranchized from the advantages of capital.

Money, of course, is a crucial feature of the novel, and is one of the themes carried over from *Other People*, but where it was a minor theme in the earlier novel, it is given ubiquitous presence in Self's narrative.[27] In *Other People*, money is viewed from the outside, and is defamiliarized by Mary Lamb's naïve perspective; in *Money*, though, Self is immersed in a capital economy. In a sense he epitomizes the Marxist notion of the economy as the base determinator of all the superstructural aspects of society that conditions the psychological make-up of individuals and determines personal behaviour, beliefs and relationships with others in a form of cultural Marxism suggested by the French critic Louis Althusser. As Self comments 'I am probably not alone in supposing that I am shaped by how I see things' (*M* 249). Later he questions the origins of his thoughts: 'I disclaim responsibility for many of my thoughts. They don't come from me. They come from these squatters and hoboes who hang out in my head' (*M* 267). *Money* can be seen as Althusserian in that there is no escape for Self from the capital economy, and he remains perpetually locked in the debased culture that money has produced. Even the high culture to which Martina Twain and the 'Martin Amis' who appears as a character in the book subscribe is also shown to be conditioned by the *'money monkey'* (*M* 384). Amis can hardly be described as a Marxist, but his novels of the 1980s present a world in which the late capitalist era can be seen to be determining force in characters' actions, motivations and belief systems.[28] The dehumanizing effects of monetarism also go some way to account for Amis's presentation of the people in texts as constructed, artificial 'agents', whose characteristics are in large part interpellated by the society in which they find themselves. During the era when Margaret Thatcher was claiming that 'there's no such thing as society' and Reaganomics was the dominant force in American economic policy, John Self is presented as the inevitable product of a late-capitalist emphasis on the all-powerful drives of the market economy.[29] However, *Money* takes us beyond a straightforward critique of capitalist society. For Amis value judgements about money are themselves ambiguous and the novel presents only a partial reading of the 1980s – it does not, for example, include any reference to the strong and sustained oppositional political movements to monetarism during the period. This is perhaps because Amis sees them as ineffective, but it is more likely that he wants to implicate the reader in the society that is supported by the likes of John Self. The lasting message of the text appears to be that in a democratic system people get the system they deserve, and even if not everyone is as excessive as John Self, he is emblematic of a democratic consent for that ideology. This ethical ambivalence towards the system presented in the novel is signposted in the various proposed titles for the film Self is producing – first *Good Money*, then *Bad Money*, and finally, simply *Money*, as the financial has so saturated contemporary experience that, according to Amis's bleak vision, it exceeds the possibility of a valid critical attack. As Self perceptively comments in the final italicized epilogue: '*Maybe money is the great conspiracy, the great fiction. The great addiction too: we're all addicted and we can't break the habit now*' (*M* 384).[30]

The link between economics and culture is a theme that is further pursued in the scenes detailing Self's attempts to produce a film of his life. This is partly a critical appraisal of the American film industry, but also a comment on the postmodern melding of the real and the imaginary in the construction of identity in contemporary society.[31] The ageing actor Lorne Guyland, for example (a pun on 'Long Island'),[32] is keen to be presented in the film as a virile and powerful man in the prime of life, despite his obvious anxieties about getting older. The childless Caduta Massey wants her character to be a font of fecundity, while the younger female star Butch Beausoleil wants to detract from her established filmic status as a 'dumb blonde' by playing an intellectual. Each of these characters, and indeed Self too, is trying to project an Ideal-I in the mediated world of the film and much of the comedy of the novel comes from Self's attempts to appease the conflicting wishes of these characters. It is the problems caused by the actors' concerns about how they will be portrayed that results in another writer being brought in, cueing the appearance of the character 'Martin Amis'. This metafictional plot device emphasizes the ironic distancing the text has towards Self, but it is also important to note that the 'Martin Amis' character can also be seen as an idealized projection of the 'real' author and that the relationship between Self and 'Amis' is more complicated than it at first appears. The plot for the film is based on Self's life, but this is the source for irony in three ways. Firstly, Self, like the actors he is trying to employ, is also in the business of fantasizing his real life to make it appear to be more interesting and commercial. Secondly, it turns out that Self's knowledge of his own life is undercut by the revelation that his real father is not Barry, but Fat Vince, the bar manager of Barry's pub. Thirdly, and adding to the blurring of the real and fictive elements of the plot, is the fact that the production of the film itself turns out to be a fantastic scam undertaken by Fielding Goodney (the film's co-producer), in cahoots with Doris Arthur, set up to fleece Self of considerable amounts of real and imaginary money, leaving him bankrupt. The metafictional devices, therefore, are absolutely appropriate in a novel that emphasizes the way in which contemporary Western society is based on a number of interacting constructions and false narratives.

Self is finally offered a way out of his overly excessive lifestyle in the relationship he begins with Martina Twain, a woman he had worked with before the opening of the novel and who he meets again in London. Unlikely as this relationship appears, Martina offers Self not only a stable, loving relationship, but the high-cultural background and moral fixity that is lacking in his life. However, Self remains sceptical: 'I have spent a good deal of this turbulent period being exposed to high culture by Martina Twain. Accordingly, I'm in a state of high-culture shock [...] While others look at art or read books or surrender to serious music, my mind just razzes me about money' (*M* 326). Although he recognizes the positive aspects of the potential stable relationship with Martina, in the end, Self lacks the ability and desire to embrace the life she offers:

> So I looked at Martina as she looked at Manet: the civilized pleasures and sacraments duly celebrated, with nothing pinched or overcorrect [...] The world of enough money, the world of enough. I saw all this but I didn't see its shine. Me, I liked the fool-the-eye

> stuff, the drinks, the bars, the grub, the bim at the picnic, the well-hung blonde, familiar, erotic. I saw all this. I didn't see its shine. But I saw Martina's shine: it filled her eyes, her mouth, her flesh – everything. (*M* 332)

Martina provides Self with a glimpse of an alternative lifestyle, but he is too far steeped in aggressive consumerist culture to settle for 'the world of enough money'. Self's inability to accept the potential escape into a normalized, mature and committed relationship is paralleled by Martina's dog Shadow who when released from his lead on the streets of New York decides to 'cut and run uptown' prompting Self to consider: 'I had a dire certainty that my fate was closely bound up with the dog's, that with Shadow gone I too would be back on Twenty-Third Street among the human canines' (*M* 337). When Selina comes back on the scene he 'automatically' heeds her call, sleeps with her, and when discovered by Martina realizes that Selina, like several of the other characters in the novel, has been in the business of duping him.

Although most of the novel serves to distance Self's 'private culture' from a normalized and accepted culture, the ending of the novel emphasizes the idea that Self and by implication the author and the reader are part of the same system that has produced Self's type. This is achieved by reducing the ironic distance from Self that is sustained during most of the novel. The dénouement involves a chess game between Self and 'Martin Amis' in which the former is 'zugzwanged' by the latter, a chess scenario in which one player is placed in a situation in which whatever move they make will result in their losing the game. This shows Amis returning to the idea that authors wield absolute power over the characters they create. The crucial difference between the two novels covered in this chapter, however, is that in *Other People* there is the sense that Prince allows Mary/Amy to have a free existence beyond his scribing of her; whereas in *Money*, Self appears to continue to exist beyond the author's attempts to kill him off. This can be seen in the final italicized section of the novel, after the apparent suicide of Self. In fact, attentive readers will have noticed that another metafictional intrusion occurs in the very final section of the non-italicized part of the novel. The suicide note alluded to in the novel's subtitle, and presented in this section, is addressed

'To Antonia', a name that has not appeared in the novel before, other than in the dedication, which in conventional fiction would be presumed to lie outside the fictional world of the novel. At this moment in this very metafictional of texts knowledge of the 'real' life of Martin Amis is crucial. During the period in which Amis was writing *Money* he was married to Antonia Phillips, to whom the epigram is presumably addressed. Given the inclusion of an Antonia in this end section of the novel, it becomes unclear to whom the 'I' belongs. Is it Self, as the reader would initially presume given the first-person framework of the rest of the novel? Or is it 'Martin Amis'? In this latter reading, not only is Amis a metafictional entrant but so is his 'real-life' wife Antonia, the person implored not to 'go into the bedroom' (*M* 380). The ending thus becomes ambiguous in terms of who it is who attempts suicide, and whether they succeed. What appears to happen in fact is that the two characters are incorporated into the same figure, suggesting that Self is not external to Amis but is part of his psyche, a kind of excessive id to Amis's corrective superego. In an ideological and structural sense this carries the implication that the ironic distance the reader has felt towards Self's excessive behaviour throughout the novel is undercut. After all, ironic distance relies on a shared agreement between author and implied reader of their superior position with respect to the object of the irony. As with *Dead Babies*, a form of postmodern satire is at play here, in which the implied correct way to behave is itself found to be insubstantial and mobile.

This ambiguous ending is further complicated in that Self appears to live on beyond his appointed death in an italicized epilogue, a metafictional ploy that appears to unsettle the author as much as it does the reader:

> *I don't see Martin Amis anymore because I owe* him *money, in a sense* [. . .] *Mind you, I did see him once. I was down the drinker* [. . .] *Our eyes met as he came through the door: he looked at me in the way he used to before I ever met him – affrontedly, with a sudden pulse in the neck* [. . .] *'Hey what are you doing here?' he asked. 'You're meant to be out of the picture now.' I just glanced over my shoulder and said* [. . .] 'Fuck *off out of it.' In the bendy mirror behind the bar I saw him leave, woodenly, stung, scared.* (*M* 388–9)

The implication is that Self is not simply a fictional character put in play for the duration of the novel, but has now entered the 'real' society from which the novel has emerged: the 'bendy mirror' representing this blurring of a real image and the reflection of that image in a mediated form. Metaphorically then, Self's existence transcends the conventional boundaries of the literary fiction in which he is placed. This example of narrative metalepsis, in which the frame of a work of literature is broken by having a fictional character step into the real world or an author enter his or her own fiction, is a subsection of metafiction that particularly seemed to interest Amis during this period. The metaleptic twist at the end of *Money* serves to foreground the relationship between the real and the fictional and acts as an examination of the conventions of realism as a literary mode. In this novel, the author shows that the fiction he has created dovetails with the reality he has observed and which has formed the source material for that fiction. The examination of the ontological axioms of fiction is explored further in his next novel, *London Fields*.

4

Millennial Fictions: *London Fields* and *Time's Arrow*

'*everything* is called *Millennium* just now' (*LF* ix)

If *Money* represents the arrival of Amis as a major British writer, then his next two novels served to cement the reputation, albeit with a certain level of controversy that has become the normal critical response to the publication of a new Amis novel. *London Fields* and *Time's Arrow* concern themselves with cultural contexts and anxieties that span the period from the beginning of the Second World War to the end of the twentieth century. *London Fields* approaches the theme of apocalypse by turning both backwards and forwards from the moment of its publication in 1989. Written during the latter stages of the Cold War, this apocalyptic vision is profoundly influenced by Amis's concerns with nuclear capabilities and a lack of faith he shows in politicians resisting the desire to use them at some point in the future. In this novel, Amis is at the height of his imaginative and stylistic skills, and its complex plot and satirical awareness of both popular and serious literary conventions mark it out as one of his finest novels. Nevertheless, it created controversy mainly due to the accusation that it promoted sexist attitudes to women in the creation of its central *femme fatale*, Nicola Six. *Time's Arrow* also courted controversy, mainly with respect to the stylistic attitude the novel takes towards its main subject matter: the Holocaust. The main reason for the criticism related to a disjunction between form and subject matter. Postmodernism, by the early 1990s, was perceived to be an intellectual movement or literary style that tended to be playful, mocking and irreverent toward distinctions between high and low forms:

it was a style that was not deemed appropriate for dealing with subjects such as the Jewish Holocaust.[1] Nor did the Holocaust seem to be appropriate subject matter for the kind of novel that Amis was at this moment famous for producing. *Time's Arrow* adopts a narrative experiment that presents the novel's events in reverse order, a technique that produces startling juxtapositions of comic situations with the horror of the concentration camps, often with an unexpected lyrical poignancy. In what was becoming a recognizable theme in Amis's fiction, the narrative manipulates the reader's feelings towards the central character, and as a whole is far from being a flippant response to the wartime atrocities but is rather a prime example of the way in which postmodern literary techniques can be very effective in producing politically-engaged fiction.[2]

LONDON FIELDS

Amis's sixth novel, published in 1989, is set in the London of 1999 and, like *Dead Babies,* can be seen as a projection of the state of Britain ten years hence. It combines a parodic reflection of the traditional hard-boiled crime novel, with a commentary on the state of the nation, or rather where the nation might very well be heading. In a prefaced note to the novel, signed 'M. A.', the reader is told of several alternative titles that were considered, one of which was 'Millennium', and the idea of a forthcoming apocalypse is one of the dominant tropes in the novel. The narrative is told by Samson Young, a New York writer who has negotiated an apartment swap in London with one Martin Asprey, a very successful British writer. We never meet Asprey, but the M. A. of his initials suggests a connection with Martin Amis himself and continues Amis's interest during this period in the ontological nature of authors, authorship and authority, and also makes the 'M. A.' of the introductory note ambiguous. Samson is ostensibly writing about the characters he encounters in the real world of the novel and as he states on the first page, he has been given the plot from real life, as his 'tears of gratitude stain the page' on which he is writing. He also suggests that the story will be a murder story, and that 'I know the murderer, I know the murderee. I know the time, I know the place. I know the motive (*her* motive) and I know the means' (*LF* 1). This apparently found story is presented in a series of chapters with alternate interludes detailing Samson's observations of the people he is writing about and the events that entwine them.

The murderer, murderee and foil appear to relate to the three main characters to be recorded in Samson's novelization of the situation he finds himself in, although the designation of roles is found not to be as straightforward as the opening three chapter titles seem to imply. Firstly, there is Keith Talent, a white, working-class man, who is a misogynist, casually racist and who makes a living through a series of petty-criminal schemes. Then there is Guy Clinch, the foil, an upper-middle-class 45-year-old, married to Hope, and with an exaggeratedly disruptive baby, Marmaduke. We learn early on that Guy 'wanted for nothing and lacked everything' and that he is currently 'wide open' emotionally (*LF* 27), laying the ground for the appearance of the third main character, Nicola Six, with whom Guy falls hopelessly in love. It is the character of Nicola Six around which the plot circulates with an ominous inevitability, and it is the representation of her as an exaggerated *femme fatale* that drew much of the criticism Amis received for the novel in relation to its sexual politics.[3] Nicola has the gift of premonition, and it is in the foreknowledge of her murder that she is provided with a disturbing power over the other characters. She is able to manipulate Keith and Guy (and also, it emerges, Samson) by acting out their fantasies. She is less a representation of a realistic character and more of a cipher – a postmodern performance that dupes those around her. As Susan Brook describes, she is 'the form of the postmodern text, deconstructing the distinction between the real and the fictional'.[4] The four main characters (including Samson) first meet in the Black Cross, a pub on Portobello Road in west London, and it is the four points of the cross that represent the axis of the plot.

The setting for these characters is a bleak view of Britain's capital on the eve of the millennium, and the sense of impending doom extends beyond the characters to the society to which they belong. Published in 1989, the novel still reveals something of the Cold War angst about the proliferation of nuclear weapons and the inevitability of a future nuclear holocaust, a theme that Amis had pursued in the volume of short stories *Einstein's Monsters* published the year before. In the introduction to that volume, titled 'Thinkability' Amis writes:

> How do things go when morality bottoms out at the top? Our leaders maintain the means to perform the unthinkable. They contemplate the unthinkable, on our behalf. We hope, modestly enough, to get through life without being murdered; rather more confidently, we hope to get through life without murdering anybody ourselves. Nuclear weapons take such matters out of our hands: we may die, and die with butcher's aprons round our waists. (*EM* 6)

Amis goes on to consider the ethical implications of a world system that relies on the Mutually Assured Destruction policy of nuclear proliferation, and the collective psyche produced by living with imminent mass death and murder. He pursues these themes in five short stories including 'The Immortals' which imagines a post-nuclear world in which humanity is on the point of annihilation, told by a narrator who stands outside of humanity but has coexisted as a kind of conscience or devilish figure.

In *London Fields* this theme is grafted onto Nicola Six's narrative, who in a sense dramatizes the desire for selfdestruction that Amis implicitly identifies with the MAD logic of the Cold War nuclear stand-off. Nicola's imaginary childhood friend is Enola Gay, the name of the Boeing B-52 that dropped the atomic bomb on Hiroshima in 1945, who has an imaginary baby called Little Boy, the nickname the pilots gave to the bomb. The bombs dropped on Japan mark, for Amis, the establishment of a new philosophical and psychological epoch, in which humanity has for the first time the power to annihilate itself. For humanity to end in a nuclear holocaust is therefore a form of species-wide suicide. This context thematically parallels Nicola's wish to destroy herself, and thus her need to identify a killer to carry out the deed. For most of the text, the suggestion is that this job will fall to Keith, a role that is in keeping with this particularly nasty example of humankind, and therefore provides a somewhat comforting logic. For nuclear holocaust to take place, it is implied that a particularly nasty agent needs to arise: a dictator or crazed world leader. That Samson turns out to be the murderer brings home the absurdity of the nuclear situation. That nuclear weapons have been adopted by democratic governments in the West suggests that we are all implicated in the inevitable end to which they point. Where Keith can be castigated for his behaviour from a position of moral superiority, Samson cannot, as the reader has spent over 400 pages being persuaded that his perspective is closer to our own.

The sense of impending global catastrophe is paralleled with the local politics of Britain, in which a decade of Thatcherism appears to have left the country on the verge of some kind of inevitable conflagration. As in several of his other novels, Amis draws on tropes and metaphors drawn from astronomy, and these have particular relevance to the inevitable trajectory of the murder plot. One particular astronomical metaphor is the black hole, and again it is with Nicola that this trope is most closely associated. This is partly related to the dark inevitability of apocalypse, an astronomical phenomenon that includes 'the *event horizon,* where spacetime collapsed, the turnstile to oblivion beyond which there was only one future, only one possible future'. As Samson informs the reader, 'She's it. She's the naked singularity. She's beyond the black hole' (*LF* 76). Amis also develops the symbolism in relation to Nicola's body and what appears to be her embarrassing secret about her desire for anal sex. The novel juxtaposes the idea of the astronomical black hole with this dark centre of Nicola's sexuality, but significantly Samson learns of her 'secret' when he finds her diaries, which suggests that this is one of the ways she lures Samson into her self-destruction, in a similar way to her manipulation of Keith and Guy. That it is revealed that Nicola has purposely allowed Samson to find her diaries suggests the attraction to anal sex is his more than hers.

Alongside the astronomical and meteorological metaphors, another important idea in *London Fields* is the end of love, and indeed the metafictional note at the beginning of the novel suggests that 'The Death of Love' has been rejected as one of its alternative titles (*LF* ix). Love's demise, however, is broadened beyond the novel's characters to suggest a general critique of contemporary culture, where it is no longer an authentic emotion, but one that can be constructed and exploited. This can be seen most notably in Nicola's manipulation of Guy, but is also of relevance to Keith, of whom she observes that 'the capacity for love was extinct in him' (*LF* 72). In the complex layering of plot, it is always difficult to identify which of Nicola's thoughts are genuine, or are part of Samson's reading of her; however, it seems likely that Nicola rejects Keith as her murderer because of his incapacity to love as 'she had always felt love in some form would be present at her death' (*LF* 72). It is, however, equally valid to imagine Nicola has identified Samson as her murderer from the outset, at the moment in which they all meet in the Black Cross.

Much of the novel, then, is taken up with the working out of the complex plot of deception and misunderstanding of the motives of characters, but, as with all of Amis's novels, there is also a fair amount of critical commentary of contemporary society. *London Fields* follows on from *Money* in its implicit critique of 1980s monetarism. Although Samson's narrative is politically ambivalent, the novel as a whole offers a critique of the projected effects of a decade of social policy that laid responsibility on the individual rather than society. Nevertheless, the novel attempts to establish a moral outlook that centres responsibility on the individual as well as society; as Samson comments at one point in relation to the historic causes for Keith's character: 'But we mustn't go too far back, must we, we mustn't go too far back in anybody's life. Particularly when they're poor. Because if we do [. . .] then nobody is to blame for anything, and nothing matters, and everything is allowed' (*LF* 180). Nevertheless, the sense in which Keith is as much a product of society as a freely-acting individual also comes out at moments in the text. At one point Keith is described as having a 'tabloid face. Shock. Horror. You just read his flickers and frowns' (*LF* 80). In effect Keith's character is mediated through the lowest forms of contemporary media; he is written as a stereotype, but the stereotype is not of Amis's making, it is representative of the broader culture to which Keith belongs. And in a sense this is the way all the characters are to be read in *London Fields*, not as realistic representations of contemporary people, but characters that are already mediated into stereotypes. This postmodern aspect of the text is what some of those critics that focus on the politics of representation often overlook.[5] However, one of the problems here is that the novel does not go out of its way to acknowledge these stereotypes as constructed, and some of the misogynist (and racist) comments in the novel cannot be simply explained as confined only to Samson Young's perspective.

In terms of class, Amis's approach is primarily cultural, and similar to Pierre Bourdieu's interpretation of class as identified in terms of what the latter calls 'cultural capital'.[6] In the relationship between Keith and Guy what represents cultural capital is clearly indicative of a general blurring of the relationship between traditional understandings of the distinction between high and low culture. In one sense Guy is attracted by the otherness of Keith's familiarity with London working-class culture; it is part of his desire to move away from his privileged background. Keith's culture is primarily summed up by darts and TV, and perhaps more accurately by darts *on* TV – representing the zenith of his ambitions. He also has a penchant for pornography, and it is made clear that this form of mediated sexuality is valued far more highly than the various real sexual relationships he has with women. It is this aspect of Keith's personality that Nicola identifies and why she decides to lure him by making him his own personal porn movie.

Keith and Guy, then, are presented as exaggerated emblems of the social classes to which they belong, revealed ironically in their attitude to money. Keith manages to procure huge amounts of it through his various criminal activities, but he never has any to hand, mainly due to a heavy, and highly unsuccessful, gambling habit, which in turn fuels his constant desire to acquire more. Guy on the other hand is very rich, but despises money and at one point speculates: 'Was there any clean money on earth? Had there ever been any? No. Categorically. Even the money paid to the most passionate nurses, the dreamiest artists, freshly printed, very dry, and shallowly embossed to the fingertips, had its origins in some bastardy on the sweat shop floor' (*LF* 255). As with Amis's previous novels, money is an integral part of the social critique in *London Fields*, but it is suggested that the individualism and monetary policies of the Thatcher years, from the standpoint of the novel's setting a decade in the future, are responsible for a kind of terminal decline in contemporary culture. Indeed, as Philip Tew has suggested, *London Fields* as a novel of the late 1980s is responding to a very different set of social, cultural and economic factors than *Money*: 'In *London Fields*, the entire world remains in crisis – a crisis more fundamental than the Thatcherite-Reaganite excesses of the 1980s [in *Money*] – because its continuation is threatened'.[7]

This world of extremes is peopled by exaggerated characters – grotesques that go beyond stereotyping to encapsulate the core of a particular kind of identity. In this way, Keith Talent is presented as the essence of a new working-class masculinity; Guy as a middle-class male whose one-time automatic acceptance of a patriarchal role is thwarted by his wife Hope's self-sufficiency and his child Marmaduke's monstrously slapstick control over his parents. These characters are comic in their grotesquery; however, they reveal aspects of the contemporary culture from which they emerge. Guy in particular is presented as a lost character who is desirous of a new engagement with firstly working-class culture in the figure of Keith, and secondly the idea of a renewed romantic and patriarchal relationship with Nicola. The relationship between Guy and Keith is interesting in this context and reveals a homosocial competition between the two masculinities fuelled by Nicola's manipulation of them.[8] As Tew argues, Amis's 'self-evident class perspective' makes this an unequal critique; nevertheless, as a pairing they each reveal aspects of a contemporary crisis of masculinity fuelled by the rise of feminism in the decades leading up to the novel. That each is easily manipulated by Nicola's apparent donning of recognized images of femininity reveals part of this desire in both men for pre-second-wave feminist gender relationships.

It is in this final aspect that the text returns to the themes of authorship and control. Once Nicola and Samson have mutually destroyed themselves in the murder-murderee plot, the two letters that Samson leaves (one for Mark Asprey, one for Kim Talent) produce an ambiguous exit from the text. In a metafictional twist, Samson implores Asprey, when he returns to his flat, to be his literary executor and to destroy the 'full confession' that the novel Samson has been writing about Nicola, Guy and Keith now represents. It is possible that Asprey does not honour the plea and that the novel the reader has just finished is ostensibly published by the returning author. Samson's last words to Asprey, 'You didn't set me up. Did you?' leaves that possibility open to speculation. The final note is to Kim Talent, and reveals Samson's one worthwhile action: he has tried to ensure, through Guy, that the child will be protected from further abuse. In this sense the novel baulks at the absolute death of love suggested by its stalled title, although the love that remains is left as a slender and precarious thread in this novel of impending apocalypse.

TIME'S ARROW, OR THE NATURE OF THE OFFENCE (1991)

If *London Fields* traces a trajectory towards the black heart of apocalypse and death then *Time's Arrow, or The Nature of the Offence* ostensibly reverses the direction. Nevertheless, Amis does not imbue this reversal with a corresponding sense of escape from a bleak vision of humanity. The novel effectively tells the story, backwards, of Odilo Unverdorben, a doctor involved in the atrocities at Auschwitz, and his escape from Germany after the war to Italy and Portugal, and then for several years in the United States. In this later part of Odilo's life, which because the story is told in reverse the reader is given first, Odilo has a series of pseudonyms: Tod T. Friendly, John Young and Hamilton de Souza, that serve to mask his true identity. Tod appears at the opening of the novel as waking from death, and the first part of the novel details his body's gradual amelioration and working backwards into a professional life as a doctor in the mid-American town of Wellport. The text then tells of his life in New York as John Young, where he meets and establishes a relationship with Irene, and has several affairs with other women, and his career moves from being a doctor to a hospital orderly. The narrative then follows the main character back to Europe and the short spell he spent as Hamilton de Souza in Portugal, his affair with the maid Rosa, and then details his escape from Germany via Czechoslovakia and Italy. This section implicates the Catholic Church's involvement in securing the escape of Nazis after the war, presented in the character of Father Duryea, who aids him in finding a new identity. The momentum of the narrative thus drives us to the figure of Odilo Unverdorben and it is in this section of the novel that we get the dark irony of the phrase

'The world is going to start making sense' (*TA* 124). In the reverse logic of the events, the Holocaust is presented as a reclamatory process whereby people are given back life by the actions of beneficent doctors.

This reverse narrative offers potential for comedy, and it was this juxtaposition of highly serious subject matter with what could be construed as a flippant stylistic approach that resulted in the novel gaining criticism from a number of reviewers and critics.[9] James Buchan, for example, attacked Amis for profiting from the Holocaust.[10] However, as Will Self points out in an interview with Amis a few years after the publication of the novel, the adverse criticism was largely unfair and perhaps oddly tended to be led by British reviewers, whilst there was very little criticism from Jewish writers and critics.[11] As many of the reviewers noted, the reverse narrative technique is not unique, and perhaps the closest precursor is Kurt Vonnegut's *Slaughterhouse-Five* which also focuses on one of the darker episodes of the twentieth century – the firebombing of Dresden by allied air forces in 1944. As with Vonnegut, Amis's adoption of this distinctive style serves not to diminish the importance of the Holocaust, but to provide a fresh analysis of a subject that has had many treatments.

One of the effects of the backward narrative is to heighten the tension, as the narrative moves on 'a terrible journey, towards a terrible secret' (*TA* 12). This can only work because of the adoption of a split between the central character and the narrative voice that seems to be simultaneously inside the character and observing from above. This is a subsection of the category of internal monologue, but an interesting variation, in which the self is divided between the character undergoing the events, backwards, and the narrator describing them forwards. The narrator is part of the textual representation of events, while the character (Tod when the novel opens) is experiencing them in the corporeal world of the narrative. This narrator appears to be unaware of Tod's memories, but he does have access to his dreams, which are even more ambiguous than normal dreams, in that the narrator is not aware of the memories as the narration has not yet reached the events that are influencing them. To approach this in Freudian terms, the manifest content of the dream can be described, but their latent meanings are as yet obscure.[12] This causes the narrative consciousness to question repeatedly its existential relationship with Tod: 'what is the sequence of the journey I'm on? What are its rules [. . .] Where am I heading?' (*TA* 14). This also implies a removal of free will in that the inevitable return to the past is incontrovertible.

One of the effects achieved by the reverse narrative is to increase the poignancy of the Holocaust, particularly in the description of the gas chambers, where men, women and children begin as stacked bodies and are then brought back from the dead by the removal of the Zyklon B, the job for which Odilo is responsible. This of course fixes Odilo as central to the events in Auschwitz and is confirmed when it is revealed that he has amassed huge amounts of gold which he 'supplies' for the 'Jews' teeth' (*TA* 130). The distance here between the naivety of the narrator's commentary and the implied horror of Odilo's actions serves to intensify the dark absurdity of Auschwitz. In a way, Amis's deployment of the experimental technique evades the danger that overfamiliarization with the subject might cause due to several treatments in both popular and serious cultural forms during the period from the end of the war.[13]

The defamiliarizing effect of the narrative reversal also serves to develop other themes in the novel. Comic inversions abound when everyday actions are described backwards, such as eating, defecating and sex. Take, for example, this description of playing tennis: 'Tennis is a pretty dumb game, I'm finding: the fuzzy ball jumps out of the net, or out of the chicken wire at the back of the court, and the four of us bat it around until it is pocketed – quite arbitrarily, it seems to me – by the server' (*TA* 20–1). As with *Other People*, the defamiliarizing can also be used to supply satirical commentary on contemporary culture, for example in the description of the 'kindness' of pimps:

> Where would the poor girls be without their pimps, who shower money on them and ask for nothing in return? Not like Tod and his tender mercies. He just goes around there to rub dirt in their wounds. And backs off quick, before the longsuffering pimp shows up, and knocks the girl into shape with his jewelled fists. As he works, the baby in the cot beside the bed will hush its weeping, and sleep angelically, secure in the knowledge that the pimp is come. (*TA* 39–40)

The technique also suggests existential questions about the trajectory of human life, its beginnings and ends, as in the description of birth where: 'Two go in. But only one comes out. Oh, the poor mothers, you can see how they feel during the long goodbye, the long goodbye to babies' (*TA* 41). This last example works on the level of the comic inversion, but also provides an ominous projection to the secret to which the narrator is heading concerning Tod's past (and his own future).

One of the other topics treated in the novel is the process of ageing, again comically approached through the reverse narrative. As the narrator notes: 'Every day, before the mirror, as I inspect Tod's humanity – he shows no sign of noticing the improvement. It's almost as if he has no point of comparison. I want to click my heels, I want to clench my fist: *Yes*. Why aren't people happier about how great they're feeling, relatively? Why don't we hug each other all the time, saying, "How *about* this"' (*TA* 52). The backwards narrative allows the insight into how lucky we are in the present and that ageing will almost inevitably make things worse. This view is the privilege of hindsight – the ability to look back on one's former self and think it was better then. As Amis has commented in interview, this theme was born of the idea of mid-life crisis and the recognition of the reality of one's death and the inevitability of the decline of the body as one ages.[14]

As well as the dark figure of the doctor, the other significant feature that haunts Tod's dreams is the 'bomb baby'. Babies and their defencelessness form a central theme in the novel but their power over Tod's psyche is expressed especially in his dreams. The importance of babies is not fully realized until the central sections but the theme supplies a motif and rhythm in the early sections of the novel. Amis develops a trope that focuses on the power of babies to impact on the conscience of adults: 'You naturally associate babies with defencelessness. But that's not how it is in the dream. In the dream, the baby wields incredible power' (*TA* 54). In the dream, the baby is 'like a bomb' (*TA* 55). This power resides in the effect the baby dreams have on Tod's conscience, to represent the terrible guilt he has over his past actions.

What the series of defamiliarizations begin to do, as they should, is persuade the reader to contemplate 'the nature of the offence' in forward, 'real' time. This can be seen poignantly in the symbolic use of doctors in the text. In the descriptions of the events in the concentration camp, the doctors appear to be fulfilling their *raison d'être* in that they are saving people's lives, and generally ameliorating their existence. In the reverse logic the world does indeed start 'making sense' (*TA* 124). This contrasts with the description of doctors in Tod's part of the narrative in the earlier sections of the book in the United States. The power of doctors is hinted at throughout the text, as they are presented as kinds of shamen with power over death, and as life's gatekeepers (*TA* 11), looked at by other people with deference, respect and hope. However, the image of a more sinister doctor haunts Tod's dreams: 'presiding over the darkness out of which I had loomed there was a figure, a male shape, with an entirely unmanageable aura, containing such things as beauty, terror, love, filth, and above all power' (*TA* 12). This figure with 'white coat' and 'black boots' disrupts the conventional image of a God-like figure supposedly encountered by people on the point of death, replacing it with one associated with power and, potentially, evil.

As well as providing set pieces, the narrative technique of writing the story backwards also produces interesting and unconventional approaches to the act of reading itself. Roland Barthes has identified that one of the functions of narrative is to provide a deferral of explanation and meaning, which in turn produces the suspense that drives the narrative forward, which he calls the hermeneutic code.[15] In *Time's Arrow*, the suspense is achieved by discovering what has already happened. This is an aspect of certain kinds of narrative, where the narrator is relating the story from the present and going back to the past. But in most novels of this type, this shift in temporal perspective happens only occasionally in a narrative that tends on the whole to move forwards, for example in Pip's narration of his life in *Great Expectations*. *Time's Arrow* is substantially different in that this mode is sustained throughout the novel. So the dual time of the long event that is looming from Tod's past, and his immediate experiences, are both narrated backwards. This works particularly in the book's unique representation of dialogue, in which exchanges are reversed, but the syntax of each individual speech sentence moves forward. This disrupts the conventional way of reading, and provides it with an internal rhythm that is substantially different from virtually all other novels. Readers are forced to cope with this in different ways. One response is to read them first as presented in the text, and then to read them again back up the page in the order they would have appeared in a conventional, forward conversation. This achieves a disruption to the linear flow of the narrative, as it tends to encourage the reader to read backwards in cycles, suspending the move forwards. This is a technical device, but it is wholly appropriate to the subject matter, at least in the first half of the book, in which the reader is projected towards the dark secret at the heart of Tod's past, but the nature of the offence is clearly so terrible, that an unsettling hesitancy is written into the very fabric of the narrative. The reader encounters the dark secret in very short steps and is repeatedly persuaded to pause and reflect, a technique which increases the power of the eventual revelations.

As noted earlier, the novel was controversial because of its adoption of this playful postmodern style for its examination of the Holocaust, but another area of problematic representation has been overlooked by critics: Amis's penchant for essentializing national and racial characteristics. This is a feature of Amis's works that appears in several of his novels, non-fiction, and public comments, perhaps most notably in his reading of Muslims in the period after the September attacks on the World Trade Center and the Pentagon in 2001, a controversy that is discussed in greater detail in Chapter 6. *Time's Arrow* offers a central contradiction in identifying where the Holocaust's cause lies, at times suggesting its roots are in the darker aspects of human nature, at others locating it in the German psyche. This identification of a national characteristic behind Nazism is obviously problematic in terms of the presence of resistance movements to Hitler and fascism within Germany in the 1930s and 1940s.[16] The contradiction can be seen in the following passage: 'The offence was unique, not in its cruelty, nor in its cowardice, but in its style – in its combination of the atavistic and the modern. It was, at once, reptilian and "logistical". And although the offence was not definingly German, its style was' (*TA* 176). It is in this fracture between the national as a frame of essential characteristics and as something constructed in the imagination that the text tries to understand the terrible logic behind the Holocaust.

The novel also details the way in which the Nazi system appears to focus on the psychological relationship with detritus. As Georges Bataille writes in 'The Psychological Structure of Fascism', German Nazism seemed to dwell, and take pleasure in the subversive desire to focus on human waste. According to Bataille, and following Freud, excrement is one of the things that children learn to reject, however, a desire for the attractiveness of faeces is pushed into the subconscious. It is Bataille's argument that the return of this repressed desire is one of the psychological drives fuelling the apparent love of the degradation of other humans revealed in fascism. This is placed alongside the designation in German Nazism of the mid-twentieth century of Jewish people (and other non-Aryans) as manifestations of a waste that needs to be cleansed. This 'justification' is part of the warped logic of the Holocaust that Amis taps into in *Time's Arrow*, and again foregrounds through inversion:

> The Auschwitz universe [. . .] was fiercely coprocentric. It was *made* of shit. In the early months I still had my natural aversion to overcome, before I understood the fundamental strangeness of the process of fruition. Enlightenment was urged on me the day I saw the old Jew float to the surface of the deep latrine, how he splashed and struggled into life, and was hoisted out by the jubilant guards, his clothes cleansed by the mire. (*TA* 132)

This ambivalent psychological relationship of humans to their own waste is hinted at in the consideration of the first-person pronoun in German: 'But *Ich*? It's like the sound a child makes when it confronts it's own . . . Perhaps that's part of the point' (*TA* 134). That the 'I' of the German psyche is presented as a verbal echo of the psychological foundation of fascism is perhaps linguistically interesting, but of course, is another contentious example of Amis perceiving behaviour as intrinsically related to national character.

It is in the inconsistency between identifying the Nazi atrocities as somehow part of an essential German character and the idea that Odilo is unexceptional that the central contradiction of the novel lies. This contradiction is not necessarily a flaw of the novel, but serves as a crucial question:

can the Holocaust be blamed on an ideology, whether political or national, or is it a manifestation of a darker, essential aspect of human psychology? This question, of course, haunts much discussion of the events of the mid-twentieth century in subsequent art, literature and cultural theory, and it is a theme to which Amis returns in a different context in his 2006 novel *The House of Meetings*.

5

Mid-Life Crises: *The Information* and *Night Train*

> 'This whole thing is a crisis. The whole mess is a crisis of the middle years' (*I* 62)

Amis's fiction has always been concerned with exploring the ways in which social and cultural movements and ideologies impact on the construction of people's identities, morals and behaviour. *The Information* and *Night Train* are both concerned with characters in periods of crisis, who are forced to reflect upon the way their individual identities are affected and changed by social experiences. Although written only two years apart in the 1990s, the two novels are stylistically very different. *The Information* is a dark comedy involving two novelists, both of whom are entering middle age: Richard Tull, an unsuccessful writer who represents the novel's main perspective, and Gwyn Barry, his more successful long-time friend. The novel deals with questions of literary value through Tull's increasing jealousy of Gwyn's successes with writing, money and women. *The Information* shows a return to the literary landscape in which Amis is most confident, contemporary London, and can be identified as the third novel in a loose trilogy with *Money* and *London Fields*. The novel's narrative framework is less self-conscious than those of his previous novels, and produces a more direct address between author and reader through the use of a third-person narrative voice. A critical distance is established between the narrator and Richard, but this is far less than that which exists in most of Amis's previous works, and the reader's empathy is greater with Richard than probably with any other character in Amis's fiction, until perhaps Des

Pepperdine in *Lionel Asbo*. This has led James Diedrick to suggest that the novel is Amis's most autobiographical since *The Rachel Papers*, although the idea of autobiography cannot be straightforwardly attached to Richard's narrative, and indeed Amis's own relationship with literary culture can be seen as an amalgam of the Richard and Gwyn characters.[1]

Night Train is a bleaker novel that, unusually for Amis, has a female narrator. However, the narrative of Detective Mike Hoolihan is less convincing and less provocative than that of the other narrators Amis has produced: the control of the American Cop idiom is consistent, but less provoking than a Charles Highway, John Self or Samson Young. Any experiment with the female voice is largely negated by the emphasis on the masculine aspects of Hoolihan's character (as indicated by her first name). The 'otherness' of the voice is marked more by the American working-class idiom it deploys, than by any distinct femininity. Despite the formal differences between the two novels covered in this chapter both have a shared theme in the exploration of a central character who is going through a mid-life crisis – one in which they are forced to readdress their lives and belief systems and to question their place in the universe, and the astronomical imagery that pervades both these novels supplies a post-human landscape against which the meaning of individual lives is explored.

THE INFORMATION (1995)

The Information follows the story of Richard Tull, who as the novel opens is celebrating (or rather bemoaning) his fortieth birthday. Richard is a writer who has had a minor success with his first novel, but who has since fallen into obscurity due to the fact that his novels have become increasingly experimental and unreadable. He survives (just about) by producing tedious reviews and working in a largely unpaid capacity as the Books and Arts Editor of an obscure publication called the *Little Magazine*, and as the Special Director of the Tantalus Press, which specializes in vanity publishing. In practical terms he lives off his wife Gina, who is the main breadwinner and dominating force in the family, which includes their two sons

Marco and Marius. Early in the novel we learn that Gina has given Richard an ultimatum: if he cannot earn any money from his novels he has to give up writing fiction. He has managed to stall this deadline for one year, in the same way that he manages to stall other deadlines for works he has been given advances for but are either unfinished, unstarted or unconceived.

The Information is probably Amis's funniest novel and includes some of his most humorous set pieces. For example, the passage that describes Richard taking a vacuum cleaner to be repaired is high comedy of the kind that pits the heightened sensibility of the long-suffering author against the frustrations of everyday life: 'By the time he got the vacuum cleaner down into the hall Richard was sure that Samuel Beckett, at some vulnerable time in his life, had been obliged to take a vacuum cleaner in. Céline, too, and perhaps Kafka' (*I* 47). The form is the mock heroic, but framed within the context of a lapsarian contemporary culture and perhaps the main influence is again Joyce, a writer the novel refers to in the opening sections. Richard's narrative balances high literary pretensions with the frustrations of the quotidian, placing him at the lower end of the downward trajectory of literary heroes he identifies in one of his stalled projects *The History of Increasing Humiliation*, 'a book accounting for the decline in the status and virtue of literary protagonists. First gods, then demi-gods, then kings, then great warriors, great lovers, then burghers and merchants and vicars and doctors and lawyers. Then social realism: you. Then irony: me. Then maniacs and murderers, tramps, mobs, rabble, flotsam, vermin' (*I* 129). This downward trajectory also parallels the sense of the decline into old age that forms one of the other main themes of the novel.

Richard is described as a 'revenger, in what was probably intended to be a comedy' (*I* 133), and this is an apt description of the form of the novel. In terms of genre, *The Information* offers ironic allusions to the classical and Renaissance genre of the revenge tragedy, a mode that is seen to have lost its heroic context in the tawdriness of contemporary culture. As the narrator contemplates at one point, 'something has [...] gone wrong with the genres. They have all bled into one another. Decorum is no longer observed' (*I* 53). In this sense the novel is closer to *Twelfth Night* than to *Hamlet*, and Richard is in many ways a kind of contemporary Malvolio, mocked for his misplaced pretensions to high culture and romance. The object of this revenge is Richard's closest friend (and bitterest rival) Gwyn Barry, a very successful novelist who, according to Richard, writes cloyingly sentimental rubbish. Gwyn is happily married to Lady Demeter Barry (daughter of the thirteenth Earl of Rievaulx) who, to Richard's annoyance, is beautiful and wealthy and with whom Gwyn is nauseatingly in love; Richard is especially scathing of a TV programme in which Gywn has appeared called the Seven Deadly Virtues, where 'Gwyn had picked Uxoriousness' (*I* 52).

Richard embarks on a series of revenge plots against Gwyn, which become increasingly violent as the novel moves forward. Initially he tries to disrupt his peace of mind by sending him an anonymous letter suggesting there is something of unspecified interest in the *Los Angeles Sunday Times*, a voluminous newspaper with several sections that would take Gwyn hours to read through: 'He wants to do to Gwyn what Gwyn has done to him. He wants to assassinate his sleep' (*I* 91). This plan backfires, however, as Richard has first to trawl through the paper to check there is not in fact any reference to Gwyn, a process he is forced to repeat when Gwyn informs Richard in passing that he found the 'reference' by chance fairly quickly. Once this plan has failed Richard gets serious and hires the 'hitman' Steve Cousins (Scozzy) to do physical and psychological damage to Gwyn. This scenario allows Amis to introduce a series of characters that span a wide range of contemporary British urban society. Scozzy is another of Amis's exaggerated and unlikely characters and might well have taken centre stage in one of Amis's previous novels – a sociopath, who intellectualizes violence, reads a range of philosophical books, and is a virgin who gets aggressive when his peers mention sex.[2] He operates in a criminal world of violence and protection, with a range of Dickensian characters such as 13, Crash, Terry and Clasford, who are largely stereotypical representatives of black, urban London. The critique of contemporary violence in the novel has something of a slapstick nature, and retains much of the grotesquery of Amis's earlier novels in characters such as Keith Whitehead in *Dead Babies*, or Keith Talent in *London Fields*. The air of impotent masculinity that surrounds Richard contrasts with the urban culture in which he finds himself. This can be seen especially in the Warlock Sports Club, where he and Gwyn go to play tennis and snooker. This 'masculine' space is representative of male culture, and male rivalry more generally: 'All men are eternally confronted by this: other men, in blocs and sets. Equipped with an act, all men are confronted by an audience which might cheer or jeer or stay silent or yawn rancorously or just walk out – giving a verdict on your life performance' (*I* 103). This generalization about male culture is, in part, what fuels Richard's envy of, and consequent revenge upon, Gwyn. However, it is clear that Richard's model of masculine revenge is operating after the gender revolution of the 1960s and 1970s and thus appears to be doomed to a comic bathos of stalled revenge and impotence.

In fact impotence is one of the main tropes of the novel and is registered in a number of ways. Richard is chronically (and comically) impotent in his sexual relationship with his wife: 'He was impotent with her every other night and, at weekends, in the mornings too [...] In the last month alone he had been impotent with her on the stairs, on the sofa in the sitting room and on the kitchen table' (*I* 89–90). This impotency is also seen more thematically in his relationship with his family, his career and his attempts to succeed in his various plots against Gwyn. Impotence is a traditional subject in low comedy, and in *The Information* it is linked to the theme of male mid-life crisis both in relation to Richard's narrative, and as a general existential reflection; as the narrator comments, echoing Wordsworth: 'Intimations of monstrousness are common, are perhaps universal, in early middle age' (*I* 64).[3] Indeed the mid-life crisis is seen as inevitable: 'Every sensitive man was allowed a mid-life crisis: when you found out for sure you were going to die, then you ought to have a crisis about it' (*I* 207).

The crisis comes to Richard most acutely at night in the form of 'information' from the unconscious: 'The information is telling me – the information is telling me to stop saying *hi* and to start saying *bye*' (*I* 124). The novel refers to the mid-life as a period of transition which ominously portends the 'other side' of old age, and this liminal time is marked by self-consciousness of the body and sexual attractiveness. At one point the novel records Richard's recognition that young women no longer look at him with sexual interest: 'Now they looked through him.

Because he no longer snagged on their DNA. Because he was over on the other side, and partly invisible. Like all the ghosts who walked there' (*I* 151). The irony, however, is that his response is to find all women more attractive, and like the speaker of Thomas Hardy's 'I Look Into My Glass', Richard finds that age does not diminish sexual longing, as he tells us, 'I still think about sex all the time' (*I* 197).[4] As in *Other People* mirrors play an important role as indicators of personal identity, but in *The Information*, the division of the self between inner consciousness and external appearance is focussed through the theme of ageing. As Richard notes in a passage of internal monologue: 'I still stare at my own reflection. This is the journey we all make, from Narcissus to Philoctetes – Philoctetes, whose wound smelled so bad' (*I* 197).[5]

The formal nature of the novel marks a departure for Amis in that he moves away from the first-person narratives that had been his stock in trade through most of his previous novels (the exception being *Dead Babies*). The narrative voice approximates to the author and there are a few self-reflexive authorial intrusions, but nothing like the metafictional twists that Amis employs in his 1980s fiction.[6] This change in narrative framework makes *The Information* the closest of the corpus to realism, although as with all of Amis's novels, the subject matter and form in which it is treated are far from straightforward.[7] Amis appears to be aware that some of his previous novels have proved to be perhaps overly-complicated in terms of narrative reference, for he provides guidance about style for the projected reader of this novel. For example, he announces a moment in the text where the technique of interior monologue 'waives the initial personal pronoun, in deference to Joyce' (*I* 11). This signal to Joyce's modernist style is intertextual but is appropriate to both the subject matter of the novel and its main focalizer. Richard is, after all, a novelist who tends to use modernist and experimental techniques in his fiction. The narrative voice simultaneously mocks and corroborates Richard's view of contemporary culture. He is clearly seen to be old-fashioned and culturally conservative, despite his Labour-leaning politics.[8] When his new literary agent, Gal Aplanalp, attempts to clarify Richard's profile with the reading public, she suggests they market him as a 'young-fogey', although Richard rejects this on the grounds he can no longer pass as young (*I* 131). His fogeyness is registered in what appears to be his lament on shifting cultural distinctions when he is less than pleased that 'the old divisions of class and then race were giving way to the new divisions: good shoes versus bad, good eyes as opposed to bad eyes [...] different preparedness for the forms that urban life was currently taking, here and now' (*I* 50).

This last quotation also reveals a central technique in the novel and in Amis's fiction more broadly: the use of binary opposites. As discussed in Chapter 3 above, although Amis is very far from being politically Marxist, his fiction often utilizes Marxist models of culture and ideology, and the binaries in the quotation can be seen to operate with respect to dialectical thinking. In the Hegelian model (developed in terms of political economy by Marx), the dialectical process involves the confrontation of thesis and antithesis, which through rational interaction results in some form of synthesis, and which moves the argument forward. However, Amis's writing tends to stall this sense of progress, preferring to see the contemporary world as a self-defeating battle between opposites without progress. The novel sets up several oppositions: high versus low culture, success against failure, age in contrast to youth, as well as the central opposition of Richard and Gwyn. To take one of these examples, the novel explores the traditional division between high and low (or popular) literature and offsets this against class. In a passage in which Richard is flying to America he describes the differing reading matter consumed by those in Coach, Business and First class:

> In Coach the laptop literature was pluralistic, liberal and humane: *Daniel Deronda*, trigonometry, The Lebanon, World War I, Homer, Diderot, *Anna Karenin*. As for Business World, it wasn't that the businessmen and businesswomen were immersing themselves in incorrigibly minor or incautiously canonized figures like Thornton Wilder or Dostoevsky [...] They were reading trex: outright junk. Fat financial thrillers, chunky chillers and tublike tinglers: escape from the pressures facing the contemporary entrepreneur. And then he pitched up in the intellectual slum of First Class [...] and nobody was reading anything – except for a lone seeker who gazed, with a frown of mature scepticism, at a perfume catalogue. (*I* 288–9)

Here the traditional registers of class hierarchy and high and popular culture have been inverted, signalling a new aesthetic world order to match the contemporary cultural decline identified by Richard. The literary journey he records here takes place as the plane is 'getting near to America' and implies that American culture is more symptomatic of the decline.

Although, as argued earlier, the novel is not metafictional to the extent of some of Amis's earlier works, it is clearly interested in detailing the state of contemporary literature. This is implicitly identified in the juxtaposition of Richard's unreadable, experimental texts and the 'trex' that Richard identifies in Gwyn's fiction. It is part of the implicit criticism of literary culture that Gwyn's writing is incredibly successful, while Richard's struggles to find a publisher, let alone readers. In this sense, the novel could be described as an example of meta-criticism, in that it includes self-reflexive commentary on the nature of literary fiction.[9] Part of this criticism includes identifying the inherent worthlessness of a range of contemporary literary production: the depressingly wasteful bulk of writing found in contemporary journalism as indicated when Richard searches out past copies of the LA Times ('the sadness and greyness and dampness and deadness of disregarded newsprint', (*I* 94)); the depressing nature of the vanity publishing in Richard's work for the Tantalus Press; the increasingly old-fashioned *Little Magazine*; the endless reviews of literary biographies 'in which no one ever went anywhere or did anything' (*I* 41); and novels written by people who were famous for something other than writing fiction. Richard recognizes the nature of contemporary publishing when he is informed by Gal Aplanalp, the go-getting and modern agent he is put onto by Gwyn that writers need to appeal to a dumbed-down readership by having a 'signature' – a simplistic single characteristic by which they are recognized and marketed.[10] 'Is that my signature? Unenvious?' asks Richard ironically when asked to take a job writing a piece celebrating Gwyn Barry's life as a writer. The critique of the way in which writers are marketed and inevitably simplified to appeal to a mass audience goes directly against the grain of Richard's intense (though pretentious) desire to produce novels that are 'experimental'. However, Richard's writing is not set up as an antidote to the decline of literary culture: 'Modernism was a brief divagation into difficulty; but Richard was still out there, in difficulty. He didn't want to please the readers. He wanted to stretch them until they twanged' (*I* 170). When Gal tries to place his novel with a publisher, the people she gets to read the novel incur increasingly serious attacks of nausea and illness.

The mid-life crisis that Richard is experiencing is therefore projected onto literary culture generally. The fact that Richard's novels are unsuccessful is partly due to his esoteric writing style, but it is also symptomatic of a literary culture that has suffered profound decline and finds itself celebrating the material that sells rather than reflecting literary merit. This is part of the postmodern culture of which Richard, and implicitly the novel as a whole, is critical. As Richard Menke has identified, one of the central oppositions in the novel is between information that is mediated by a range of technical devices that construct or perform meaning and which ultimately signify nothing, and a deeper knowledge of the human that Richard impotently strives to uncover.[11] In the world in which Richard finds himself, quantity of information has replaced quality of writing. Crisis, then, is the basis of the novel, but this is set in sharp relief against the inconsequence of individual human lives with respect to the universe, and the comparison between the vast mathematics of astronomy and the intimacy of individual human lives serves to foreground the infinitesimal inconsequence of Richard's particular mid-life crisis. Amis's use of extended metaphors drawn from science and astronomy recalls several of his novels, but unlike *Other People* and *London Fields* the emphasis is not on its potential apocalyptic collapse, but on its enormity with respect to an individual human identity: 'When we die, our bodies will eventually go back where they came from: to a dying star, our own, five billion years from now, some time around the year 5,000,001,995. [I]t might help if we knew all this. It might help if we felt all this' (*I* 65).

Richard, then, is a realist character encountering a world that is postmodern with its fluctuating and performed identities, its removal of the traditional ordered hierarchies of class, culture and gender. He is tellingly lost in this world and increasingly appears moribund and unable to adapt. The novel then simultaneously critiques both the world in which Richard operates and his refusal to adapt to the changing nature of that world. This focus on identity crisis is a theme pursued in a different direction in Amis's next novel *Night Train* (1997).

NIGHT TRAIN (1997)

Night Train sees Amis returning to the hard-boiled American detective style that he parodied in *London Fields*, although this novel is less of a parody and more of an attempt to scrutinize the realities of police work in opposition to the romanticizing of the crime and detective genre in popular forms, especially on TV. The novel presents the investigation of the suicide of one Jennifer Rockwell, an intelligent, beautiful, happy and seemingly well-balanced, post-doctoral researcher at Chicago State University. The chief investigator and narrator of the novel is Mike Hoolihan, a character who describes herself at the opening of the novel as 'a police', a form of self-categorization that foregrounds occupation over other identity categories such as gender, class, ethnicity and sexuality. It is only by the end of the introductory paragraph that the reader learns that Mike is 'a woman, also' (*NT* 1).[12] This is Amis's only novel that has a female first-person narrator, although the gender of Mike's voice is subsumed in the occupational style of language she uses. Police and policing are thus central to the narrative, both in terms of the crime narrative that *Night Train* represents, but also, as James Diedrick has noted, in the way fiction has traditionally functioned to police the moral and ethical positions of the readership.[13] One of the themes the novel introduces is the sense of 'parallel universes', as we learn that Jennifer's boyfriend, Professor Trader Faulkner, works in the field of 'Many worlds, many minds. The interpretation of relative states' (*NT* 47). The novel emphasizes the fragmentation of groups within society who struggle to understand the motivations and discourses engaged in by others. This is seen most acutely in the distinction between the police world and the academic world as Mike's investigation unfolds in the novel: they touch and cross but they do not share a perspective on existence. The image the novel presents is of an atomized culture, a series of distinct social groups that Michel Maffesoli has termed urban tribes.[14] Indeed, the police are described by Mike as a race apart, while at the same time defamiliarizing traditional notions of race: 'All police are racist [...] and once you're there you're a member of a race called police, which is obliged to hate every other race' (*NT* 4–5). Race here is not simply ethnic, it is related to distinct social and occupational categories.

Mike's gender is subsumed in her job, and there is very little to distinguish her style of language from a male cop. Indeed she is several times mistaken for a man in the narrative, both because of her name and her physical demeanour. She is largely ambivalent to this perception and in a sense likes her gender ambiguity as revealed by the fact that she never changed her name to make it sound more feminine. Despite the ambiguity related to Mike's gender the novel does offer suggestions that there are clear distinctions between the genders in their attitudes to crime, suicide and particularly violence. Mike emphasizes that 'Murder is a man thing' (NT 11), and yet she is intrigued by suicides, earning the nickname 'Suicide Mike' from her colleagues because of her willingness to take on such cases. Indeed, one of her colleagues, Silvera, suggests that women are naturally more attuned to suicide: 'Men kill other people. It's a guy thing. Women kill themselves. Suicide's a babe thing' (*NT* 33). However, this point of view is rejected once Mike starts to look at the statistics related to suicides. It is suggested that Mike is attracted to suicides not because of her gender, but because of her past experiences. She is a recovering alcoholic, who was abused by her father from the age of 7 to 10 and was subsequently 'state-raised' (*NT* 87). Because of this she explains: 'I find love difficult' (*NT* 20), and details a list of past abusive relationships she has had with men, in which it is clear she gave as good as she got. Her current relationship with Tobe is non-abusive, but is also described as lacking any real warmth or sexual feeling.

Mike's experiences, therefore, are set in stark contrast to the actual suicide of Jennifer Rockwell, an action that disrupts the expectations of all who knew her. Jennifer is found dead in her apartment with bullet wounds to her head, and it is assumed she has taken her own life. The suspicion of foul play is subsequently raised, notably by Jennifer's father, former police Colonel Tom Rockwell, mainly because she appeared to be a happy, intelligent, beautiful woman in a loving relationship, and pursuing a career she loved. This is the stuff of the traditional crime thriller, and the first part of the novel pursues speculations about alternative solutions to the case. However, the novel is at pains to disrupt the conventional trajectory of the crime mystery and it is clear by the end of the first section that Jennifer has indeed committed suicide, a conclusion that most of those close to her find more difficult to accept than murder, including, to a certain extent, Mike. This feeling is especially acute for Tom, for whom 'any outcome, yes, any at all, rape, mutilation, dismemberment, cannibalism, marathon tortures of Chinese ingenuity [. . .] was better than the other thing. Which was his daughter putting the .22 in her mouth and pulling the trigger three times' (*NT* 41).

If Part I is concerned with establishing the circumstances and details of Jennifer's suicide, then Part II moves on to the psychological motive behind her actions. In fact, the police investigation is crucially not interested in motive, a comment that chimes with a theme that recurs in several of Amis's novels: that motivation has become difficult to fix in the context of postmodern culture. As Mike says with respect to contemporary policing: 'Give us the how, then give us the who, we say. But fuck the why' (*NT* 31). It is part of Mike's interest in suicide generally and her personal connection to Jennifer that drives the investigation from this point onwards. The police case is effectively closed, but it is her dissatisfaction with not knowing the cause of the suicide that intrigues Mike. However, the novel is keen to stress that the conventional understanding of motive is not going to be appropriate to this case. Mike rejects the 'public' need for a neat tie-up and conclusion, a desire she says is related to the TV representation of crime.[15] There are repeated references to the way in which realistic approaches to crime and media representations are at odds. As Mike says: 'With TV you expect everything to measure up. Things are meant to measure up. The punishment will answer the crime. The crime will fall within the psychological profile of the malefactor. The alibi will disintegrate. The gun will smoke' (*NT* 107). It is clear that Mike's investigation is not going to provide this neat explanation: 'what I'd find wouldn't be any kind of Hollywood ketchup or bullshit but something absolutely sombre' (*NT* 64).

Mike, however, continues to investigate several 'leads' that appear to offer some kind of motivation for Jennifer's suicide. It is discovered that she has been taking lithium, a drug prescribed for manic depression, although when Mike interviews Jennifer's physician he is unaware of this. It is also discovered that Jennifer has had a brief encounter with another man, Arn Debs, a trucker she met in a hotel called The Mallard. Another possible explanation is the fact that she has made a serious error in the calculations for a major experiment at work that has been supervised by her boss Professor Bax Denziger, a high profile 'TV' scientist. A further possible factor is her friendship with Phyllida Trounce with whom she shared an apartment and who has suffered bouts of depression and drug abuse in the past. However, all of these factors are found to be dead ends: the lithium present in her blood is shown to be very recent and not part of long-term abuse; it is suggested that she had deliberately changed the data for the experiment, and perhaps most tellingly, the relationship with Arn Debs is seen to be a playful decoy set up by Jennifer herself to throw potential investigators off the scent.[16] What Mike begins to realize is that Jennifer herself has set up all these false clues as a way of feeding the desire to explain her suicide to the loved ones she has left behind: 'As she headed towards death she imprinted a pattern that she thought would solace the living. A pattern: Something seen before. Jennifer left clues. But the clues were all blinds' (*NT* 145). Jennifer has been the author of her own crime fiction, establishing the mystery of her own death and then supplying clues as to the motivation. The unsatisfying truth that Mike discovers is that there is no rational explanation for Jennifer taking her own life and this is the serious point Amis is making about the nature of suicide.[17]

The final part of the novel is called 'Seeing' and is taken from the scientific use of the term as explained by Bax Denziger: 'The quality of the image. Having to do with the clarity of the sky. The truth is, Detective, we don't do much "seeing" anymore. It's all pixels and fibre optics and CCDs' (*NT* 91). Seeing, therefore, becomes a problematic concept in the contemporary world. As Menke identified in his analysis of *The Information*, knowledge has been replaced by digital information, and therefore the older paradigms of understanding have begun to shift. This theme is worked into *Night Train* in relation to the scientific research in which Jennifer has been engaged. Mike believes that her work was not a factor in her suicide; however, the explanation Bax provides of the nature of her research challenges this belief. Bax talks of a 'revolution of consciousness' precipitated by the cosmological investigations he and Jennifer had been working on:

> We don't act like we know it, but we're now on the edge of an equivalent paradigm shift. Or a whole series of them. The universe was still the size of your living room until the big telescopes came along. Now we have an idea of just how fragile and isolated our situation really is. And I believe, as Jennifer did, that when all this kicks in, this information that's only sixty or seventy years old, we'll have a very different view of our place and purpose here. (*NT* 93)

Jennifer has clearly been thinking deeply about the implications of this kind of discovery about the universe, and as Bax tells us she has been contemplating the nature of human existence in the face of the universe as encapsulated in the (mistranslated) quotation from the seventeenth-century French philosopher François de La Rochefoucault: 'No man can stare at the sun or at death with a, with an unshielded eye' (*NT* 95). This reported conversation between Bax and Jennifer reveals something of the thinking Jennifer was engaged in during the period before she committed suicide and suggests a deeper motivation to her actions, despite Mike's later dismissal of their importance.[18]

The 'night train' of the title can refer to a number of contexts. It has a literal context in that it refers to the train that Mike hears passing her apartment in the dark hours. But it is also a metaphor for suicide: 'Suicide is the night train, speeding your way to darkness' (*NT* 67). It also refers to the song of the same title and Tobe has recorded a compilation tape of several versions of this song for Mike, suggesting that suicide takes distinct forms for individuals. In this context the ending of the novel is ambiguous. There is perhaps the suggestion that Mike has come to the end of the case, however unsatisfactory the conclusion might be, and that she has come to terms with her need to live on despite the despair that Jennifer has observed due to the meaninglessness of life. Perhaps this is an indication that Mike is going to follow the path taken by Jennifer, perhaps not in as dramatic a way, but by returning to alcohol. The final paragraph relates that she is going back to 'Battery and its long string of dives' presumably to get drunk, and the novel has already indicated that for Mike a return to the booze is an effective death sentence.

Amis's fiction of the mid 1990s clearly demonstrates his interest in scrutinizing the nature of human existence. Both Richard and Jennifer suffer from existential crises precipitated by the work they are engaged in and, in Richard's case, by the discovery of the impending actuality of one's death. The difference in response is partly determined by the differing genres of the two novels: *The Information* emphasizes the absurdist comedy to be found in the apparent meaninglessness of human existence in the face of the enormity of the cosmos; while *Night Train* shows the tragic consequences of contemplating death too closely. The ambiguous ending of the later novel with respect to Mike represents the choice the reader is left with as a response to the startling consequences of the 'revolution in consciousness' set in motion by discovering the nature of the cosmos, and by the realization of one's mortality.

6

The Wild Dogs: *Yellow Dog* and *House of Meetings*

> 'And how weary it was, how sick and tired. For this, that. For that, this' (*YD* 337)

Amis's work in the early to middle part of the 2000s shows him exploring the related themes of masculine violence, revenge and the dehumanizing of aspects of political systems and contemporary culture. Looming over much of this writing is Amis's response to the terrorist attacks on the World Trade Center and the Pentagon of 11 September 2001. What seems to emerge from this period is a reassessment of the moral and ethical approach of his fiction writing, and arguably a move away from the postmodern playfulness of his earlier novels and towards a greater sense of realism.[1]

Yellow Dog is Amis's first twenty-first-century novel, and it takes as its themes several cultural anxieties of the new millennium. Specific targets for his satire are the British tabloid press and its celebration of sex, sport and violence (both public and domestic); the royal family; and the porn industry. The novel is an exploration of masculinity in a post-feminist world, an examination of the abuses of patriarchal power (especially through the theme of incest), and the way contemporary culture reflects a crisis of masculinity through the valorization of sex and violence. As is typical with Amis's fiction, the novel is populated with a series of grotesques, for example Clint Smoker, the stereotypically unscrupulous tabloid journalist, and Xan Meo, an actor who reverts to a model of primitive masculinity after being physically attacked by the henchmen of a London gangster with the unlikely name of Joseph Andrews.

The novel sees a return to the physical environment of *Money, London Fields* and *The Information,* and has qualities of symbolic patterning that match the best of Amis's writing. There is, however, a greater desire to establish a moral centre in this novel, a position that was rejected (or at least remained ambiguous) in the earlier trilogy of London novels.

This moral turn is also pursued in two books from this period that address the history and politics of twentieth-century Russia: *Koba the Dread: Laughter and the Twenty Million* (2002) and *House of Meetings* (2006). The former is ostensibly part two of Amis's autobiography, and focuses on the way in which the Soviet Union, and in particular the role of Stalin, has been misrepresented by a number of Amis's contemporaries and associates. As with *Experience,* the experimental approach to autobiography is apparent though it is not as successful as in the earlier work. In *House of Meetings* Amis uses the same Soviet setting and historical period, but in a much more intriguing and satisfying way.

YELLOW DOG (2003)

Yellow Dog was a long time in the writing: it was published six years after *Night Train,* representing the longest gap in his output of fiction. This was due to a number of factors, both personal and professional. Amis's autobiographical *Experience* split this time between novels and registered a clearly important aspect of his personal life at this time: the death of his father Kingsley. As discussed in Chapter 1, *Experience* has much to do with Amis's relationship with his father, both in childhood and coming to terms with his death. Concern about his father seems to have interrupted work on *Yellow Dog,* although a short story collection, *Heavy Water and Other Stories* (1998), was also published during this period and contains several of Amis's earlier works in this genre, as well as 'State of England', a story that includes some characters and themes that are developed in the later novel.[2] Amis has also commented on the way in which the events of 11 September stalled the writing of *Yellow Dog*. In an interview with Gerald Isaaman, Amis recounts how he decided to turn his attention back to the novel on 10 September 2001, but that the terrorist attacks forced him to put aside fiction for a while.[3] *Yellow Dog* does not mention the attacks specifically, but as several critics have identified and Amis has corroborated, they cast a cloud over the novel, especially in the themes of masculine violence and revenge with which it deals. Philip Tew cites the novel as indicative of the traumatological atmosphere pervading British and American culture in the period after 9/11, while both Dominic Head and Gavin Keulks see the novel's focus on masculine violence as partly coming out of the attacks.[4] James Diedrick sums up this general approach to the novel when he writes: 'The novel is not directly concerned with the September 11, 2001, terrorist attacks on New York and Washington, but the atavistic beliefs that Amis sees as having motivated them are everywhere apparent. The entire novel can be read as an anatomy of and defiant campaign against those forms of unreason that unleash the dogs of destruction.'[5]

Before discussing the way the novel approaches these themes, it is instructive to pursue Amis's writing on 9/11 during the period around the writing and publication of *Yellow Dog*. Most of this writing is collected in the volume *The Second Plane*, which includes essays Amis published in the press between 2001 and 2007, and a couple of short stories that attempt to understand the impulse behind the attacks. The story 'The Last Days of Muhammad Atta' attempts to make sense of the motivation and reasoning of one of the perpetrators of the terrorist attacks, and although the account of Atta fails to achieve the right level of authenticity, it raises an interesting connection between libido and masculine violence that is also pursued in *Yellow Dog*. In the short story, Atta's approach to women is summed up when he observes that he considers 'the blend of aggression and alarmism highly congenial' in his albeit rare dealings with them, and the suggestion is made that relief from sexual urges is found in the purity of the ideology behind the terrorist acts.[6] Amis also pursues this theme in his non-fiction writing on the subject: in a review of Ed Husain's *The Islamist* published in *The Times* in 2007, Amis suggests that after Husain recognizes the falsity of the Islamist ideology to which he succumbed as a teenager, 'sexual tension, is eased not by religious rage, but by sexual love'.[57]

This connection between masculine aggression and sexuality forms much of the thematic content of *Yellow Dog*, manifest in its complicated interweaving of four, coterminous plotlines. The first follows the experiences of Alexander (Xan) Meo, a successful actor who suffers brain damage when attacked in a London pub. The second involves an unscrupulous, but highly successful tabloid journalist Clint Smoker who begins to follow up a story related to the third main plot: the blackmailing of Henry IX, King of this alternative Britain, who receives surreptitiously-taken nude images of his 15-year-old daughter, the Princess Victoria. Above all this, literally, is a fourth plotline that intersperses the main chapters with an account of the flight of the airplane CigAir 101 Heavy across the Atlantic, which has on board the coffined body of Royce Traynor, his widow Reynolds, and the captain with whom she has been having an affair.

The novel opens in the company of Xan, a successful actor, writer and minor celebrity, happily married to his second wife, Russia Tannenbaum. The first chapter recounts him moving from a location of domestic harmony to being subjected to what at first appears to be a random attack in a bar called Hollywood in Camden.[8] It is later discovered, however, that this attack has been instigated by one Joseph Andrews, a London gangland thug, who is upset because Xan has supposedly named him in a short story he has written. This is a mistake, of course, as Xan has only used the name as an ironic reference to the eighteenth-century novel; nevertheless, this inadvertently instigates the unravelling of a complex secret relationship that ties the two characters together. Andrews is on the run from the British police and is running a lucrative pornography empire on the west coast of America, and it emerges that he is Xan's real father. The initial attack sparks a cycle of revenge and violence that is developed in the novel though an Oedipal framework.[9] The head injury Xan sustains changes his personality and he becomes uncouth and highly libidinous. Most disturbingly, he begins to develop incestuous feelings towards his daughters Billie and Sophie. This return to what is presented as a primal form of patriarchal masculinity is one of the main themes in the novel.

The attack in the Camden bar has a personal, psychoanalytic context played out in terms of an imposition of the Law of the Father (Joseph Andrews) on his son, and Xan's resistance to this process. This Freudian theme, however, extends beyond the personal and is given greater cultural resonance by Amis in an attempt to comment upon the representation of contemporary masculinities in a post-feminist world. Amis makes great efforts to emphasize the ideal, gender-equal and perhaps even feminized world Xan occupies with his wife and family immediately prior to the attack. On his way to the Hollywood, Xan muses to himself: 'I am the dream husband: a fifty-fifty parent, a tender and punctual lover, a fine provider, an amusing companion, a versatile and unsqueamish handyman, a subtle and accurate cook, and a gifted masseur who, moreover (and despite opportunities best described as "ample"), never fools around' (*YD* 5). His journey out of this world occurs on the anniversary of his divorce from his first wife Pearl, a day on which he traditionally goes to a pub, has two drinks and smokes four cigarettes, and contemplates his sons from his first marriage. This journey is presented as a move from a domestic, female space into the male environment of the pub, a gendered trajectory that is accelerated by the attack and it initiates an entry into a masculinized underworld.[10] The cultural environment he enters is shown to be psychologically sick, jaundiced in a way that permeates many aspects of contemporary society, and in particular, manifest in the representation of tabloid journalism and pornography in the other two main plotlines of the novel. In the metaphorical architecture of *Yellow Dog,* Xan is projected towards the aggressive forms of masculinity that contemporary culture promotes.

As suggested earlier, this culminates in his incestuous feelings towards his daughters. This desire is not pursued, but displaced onto the character of Karla White, a character Xan encounters half way through the text. Unbeknownst to Xan, Karla is in fact the porn-name of his niece Cora Susan, who he has not seen for a number of years, and although he seems to think he has seen her before, does not recognize her as a member of the family. Cora/Karla has been working with Andrews in his pornography business, and is tasked to lay the revenge plot on Xan. Andrews aims to have her seduce Xan and thereby both wreck his marriage and disrupt his mental state by luring him into incest. Cora/Karla's motivations are less clear cut and unconvincing. She appears to want to lay the trap with Xan as a kind of vicarious revenge on her father, who had raped her when she was a child. She also tries to convince Xan that he should have sex with his own daughter and 'introduce her to the void' because as she says 'us victims, we're not so frightened by the way the world is now: the end of normalcy. We always knew there was no moral order' (*YD* 236). Cora /Karla is clearly a problematic figure in the novel, and as Gavin Keulks has noted, her construction and performance as Karla White makes her representative of the postmodern world which in this novel is epitomized by pornography.[11] Like many of Amis's characters, the best way to understand her is not to think of her as a realistic character, but as a cipher for the over-sexualized nature of contemporary society, and in particular the sexualization of children. However, the novel also tries to suggest that Cora Susan represents aspects of a genuine humanity behind the constructed Karla. Her attempt to incite Xan to commit incest with his own daughter becomes unconvincing in this context, and her emblematic role as a target of the novel's resistance to the 'obscenification of everyday life' undermines any sympathy the reader may have for her (*YD* 335). The only hint of sympathy appears at the end of the passage in which she attempts to seduce Xan, when her mask slips for a moment: after initially claiming that victims of child abuse 'get over it', she rescinds: '"No we don't" she said. *Ob*viously' (*YD* 298). Xan, therefore, is lured towards incest by a victim of masculine violence, and towards a culture that perpetuates that violence, the point seeming to be that the cycle of abuse is revisited on the next generation. According to Amis's ethical critique of aggressive masculinity, the sickness in this contemporary debased society propels individuals towards aggressive sexual relationships.

As suggested earlier, this aspect of the novel is bound up with Amis's other writing on 9/11. In the article 'The Second Plane', published a week after the 9/11 attacks, Amis comments on the far reaching effect of the attacks on collective psychology:

> the most durable legacy has to do with the more distant future, and the disappearance of an illusion about our loved ones, particularly our children [. . .] The illusion is this. Mothers and fathers need to feel that they can protect their children. They can't, of course, and never could, but they need to feel that they can. What once seemed more or less impossible, their protection, now seems obviously and palpably inconceivable. (*SP* 7)

The sentiment here is transferred in *Yellow Dog* into Cora/Karla's warped reasoning for encouraging Xan's incestuous thoughts about his daughter, the logic being that if you cannot protect your children you may as well remove any sense of innocence they have early on. Xan, however, is able to resist Karla's advances, recovers from the effects of his head injury, and is eventually rehabilitated back into the heart of his family. The novel, then, ultimately rejects the kind of self-destructive logic promoted by Cora/Karla (and by extension Andrews). That parental love triumphs over the incestuous feelings Xan is lured towards is part of the novel's resistance against the atavistic forms of patriarchal violence and revenge that Amis feels have been unleashed by the 9/11 attacks.[12]

The critique of excessive masculinity is also registered in Clint Smoker's tabloid objectification of women as a response to his own sexual inadequacies, and his impotent attempt to reclaim male power as a reaction to the successes of second-wave feminism. Clint is an unsavoury character who nevertheless carries much of the humour of the text. In many ways he is similar to John Self in *Money*, and like Self the novel allows him a certain amount of sympathy despite his shortcomings. His main hang-up is the anxiety he has about his sexual performance, which in itself is presented as a reflection of the way in which the kind of culture to which he belongs exaggerates masculine virility and machismo to unachievable levels. Clint's misogyny can partly be explained by his feelings of inadequacy. As with many of Amis's grotesques, bad behaviour is partly the fault of the individual, but also of the culture to which that individual is subjected. It is Clint's misogyny, then, that makes him such a good journalist for the *Morning Lark*, a paper that promotes the objectification of women as its central ethos.[13] The editorial board on the *Lark* is 'Naturally [...] all-male', catering for a readership which is also exclusively male and referred to by all on the newspaper as 'wankers' (*YD* 24). This redundant all-male cultural context is parodied by Amis as representative of a new powerlessness in male expression, and the emasculation is ironically represented in the celebration of masturbation as the new prime area of male sexuality. This is most comically registered in Clint's sexual inadequacies as brought out in the electronic text exchange he has throughout the novel with the anonymous 'k8'.

Clint's bile is especially revealed in his journalistic pseudonym – the eponymous 'Yellow Dog' of the novel. Clint's journalistic pieces become increasingly dark and represent the logic of this kind of journalism – the descent into ever more shocking and debased attitudes. Towards the end of the novel Clint gets great enjoyment from writing his Yellow Dog pieces, as he finds his spiritual home in 'Fucktown', the centre of America's porn industry, where he is sent to interview various porn stars. Significantly, these interviews do not result in Clint finding an actual sex life, but they do increase the yellow bile on which his writing feeds: 'to release tension, he pounded out some Yellow Dog' (*YD* 275). Clint is eventually fired when his pornographic (and paedophilic) approach to sex results in him writing a piece on the 15-year-old Princess Victoria that goes too far even for Desmond Heaf, the jaded editor of the *Morning Lark*.

It is significant that k8 identifies that Clint's misogyny is revealed in his Yellow Dog articles and the suggestion is made that, like Joseph Andrews, Clint is repressing homosexual desires. Clint discovers at the end of the novel that k8 is a transsexual, who has 'been under the nife. but not 2 destroy – 2 cre8! i've got tits and a 2l' (*YD* 327), and Amis uses this transgendered figure to examine Clint's misogyny. K8 despises both feminine women and macho men, as revealed in her criticisms of her previous boyfriend 'Orl&do'. Although k8's gender history remains ambiguous, it is clear that she has recognized in Clint's misogynistic journalism a latent homosexuality. Beyond this, she is represented in the novel as a figure that is able to critique contemporary constructions of masculinity because she has access to the inner thoughts of both genders. She is therefore able to appeal to Clint's sexual desires but, ironically, although he makes his living by exploitative aspects of the sexual revolution, he cannot cope with some of the freedoms in sexual identity it has allowed. The discovery of k8's transgender results in the removal of Clint's fragile hold on sanity and he tares off in his car, resulting ultimately in killing himself and Joseph Andrews by crashing into the latter's house just as he has returned to Britain.[14]

The demise of Smoker and Andrews seems very much like poetic justice and serves to emphasize the logical endpoint for the residual forms of masculinity each in his own way represents. That they are killed off suggests that their attitudes towards gender can no longer survive in the post-feminist world. However, the ending has drawn criticism. Diedrick, for example, has commented on the unconvincing moralizing that Amis imposes at the end of the novel: 'What is surprising is that a novel dedicated to decentring masculinity and male power should end with so much moralizing by the novel's redeemed patriarch'.[15] I am not sure that the Xan Meo that recovers from the effects of his head injury can any longer be called a patriarch; however, Diedrick makes an insightful point with respect to the awkward moralizing with which the novel ends. This is certainly not the ambiguous and unstable satire with which Amis has become associated in novels such as *Dead Babies*, *Money* and *London Fields*, and it would appear that this desire to offer an ethical framework for reading the novel is connected to his response to the events of 9/11. In particular, this position seems to emerge from the immediate effect 9/11 had on his writing and results in his desire to identify some kind of ethical grounding to set against the debased culture he presents in *Yellow Dog*, a moral move that he rarely makes in his pre-9/11 fiction.

HOUSE OF MEETINGS (2006)

In the second half of the first decade of the twenty-first century Amis publishes two works that address the terror of the Stalinist years in the Soviet Union: *Koba the Dread: Laughter and the Twenty Million* and *House of Meetings*. The former of these is meant to represent the second instalment in Amis's autobiography but covers a more broadly social and political landscape than *Experience* as it ambitiously attempts to re-address his father's and his own generation's relationship with socialist and communist politics. In particular, it interweaves personal conversations with historical data from the Stalin years in the Soviet Union. The book is not an easy read, not only because of its subject matter but also because of the overuse of repetition to hammer home the enormity of the horror of the Stalinist purges. It tries to bludgeon the readership with an extended outrage, fuelled by an attempt to defamiliarize the statistics of the purges and emphasize the horrific behaviour of those involved. Where the work does succeed is in its account of the way in which many on the Left were guilty of turning a blind eye to some of the atrocities perpetrated in the name of the Soviet Union because of the political contexts in which the Cold War politics were fought out domestically in the West. Amis is right that the ideological confrontation of Left and Right politics in Britain (and America) resulted in the playing down of Stalinism by the Left in Britain; however, he does not give enough weight to the political contexts pertaining in Britain during that period. He is much more concerned to offer a polemic against what he sees as his generation's blind spots with respect to Soviet communism. In *Experience*, experimentation with the form of autobiography achieves a powerful articulation of an individual's life; but in *Koba the Dread*, the hectoring tone, and the attempt to attach aspects of his personal relationships with people like Christopher Hitchens and James Fenton to events in mid-century Soviet Russia is an experiment that does not really come off.

Amis provides a much more powerful account of the horrors of totalitarian regimes in fiction. As we have seen, *Time's Arrow*, in its experiment with narrative order, produces a poignant engagement with the horrors of the Holocaust, and in his 2006 novel, *House of Meetings*, Amis uses the research gathered for *Koba the Dread* to produce a harrowing fictional account of the Stalinist purges after the Second World War. The novel deals mainly with the middle part of the twentieth century, but also refers to a much broader view of Russian history, both back to the past and to the post-Communist period. The plot revolves around the unequal, 'brutally scalene' love triangle that develops between two Russian half-brothers – the unnamed narrator and Lev – and Zoya, the object of desire for both of them (*HM* 7). Zoya is Jewish and lives in the same town as the brothers in the years immediately following the war. She is a dangerously independent critic of the system and her outspokenness, not to mention her racial identity, make her a target in the climate of suspicion in the USSR during the period. However, it is not Zoya but the narrator's and his brother Lev's association with her that results in them both being arrested by the authorities. The narrator is arrested first and sent to the Siberian labour camp at Predposylov, and is surprised to discover a few years later that his brother has been sent to the same camp. The narrator is even more surprised to discover that Lev has married Zoya in the intervening period, especially given the huge discrepancy in physical attractiveness between the beautiful Zoya and the grotesque Lev.

The main events of the narrative follow this triangular relationship through the brothers' time in the camp in the period from 1948 to 1956 and then after their release at various locations in the Soviet Union. The narrative circulates around a single event that takes place on 31 July 1956 in the 'house of meetings', a secluded chalet on a mountainside near to the gulag, where the wives and partners of the inmates are allowed to visit the camp and stay for one night. The novel is organized to magnify the importance of this event by introducing it in the first chapter, waiting until the middle section of the book before there is a description of the time leading up to it and its immediate aftermath, but not revealing its central revelation until the final chapter, and only then by way of a letter that Lev has given to the narrator before he dies. For the second half of the novel, all the reader knows is that something happened in the chalet between Lev and Zoya that profoundly affects Lev to the point where he says he has 'crossed over [. . .] into the other half of my life' (*HM* 106).

The story is related by the unnamed narrator in the form of an extended letter to Venus, his America-based niece, in hindsight during a trip in 2004, when he returns as a 'Gulag tourist' to Predposylov. This set-up allows Amis to contrast contemporary Western culture with the ideologies pertaining to the USSR in the middle years of the twentieth century. Although clearly critical of the Soviet regime, the narrator is keen to emphasize that Venus's political outlook is also a form of ideology, and not, as she might assume, the normative condition against which other systems are deemed ideological. In this context, the narrator points out certain ironies of behaviour by Western youth including the desire to dress as if in poverty, to have body piercings, and forego nourishment in the form of anorexia; not to mention the high divorce rates in the West generally. These 'choices' are perceived by the narrator as absurd given the enforcement of physical debasement suffered in the gulags; when describing Venus's first boyfriends he notes: 'Looking at those boys, with their sheared heads, their notched noses and scarified ears, I felt myself back in the Norlag. Is this the invention of pain? Or a little re-enactment of the pains of the past? The past has a weight. And the past is heavy' (*HM* 57). The suggestion here is of an unconscious cultural guilt about the past, and that the penchant for self-mutilation in contemporary youth subcultures is an expression of remembrance for the atrocities of the twentieth century, and perhaps reveals an unconscious guilt amongst affluent Western youth.

As with most of Amis's novels, however, how far the reader is persuaded to agree with the views of the main narrator is ambiguous. Given his history he is bound to attract a certain amount of the reader's sympathy and confirmation of his views: he has fought against the Nazis, but is designated as a fascist and an enemy of the people in the years after the war and sent to two labour camps in the north east of Russia. He is typical of many of Amis's narrators in that his ambiguous morality serves to attract and repulse the reader at different moments. We gain access to the innermost thoughts of this victim of the Stalinist oppression, but he has also been a perpetrator of inhuman acts, most notably in his description of himself as part of a 'rapist army' in the latter stages of the war: 'in the first three months I raped my way across what would soon be East Germany' (*HM* 26). This behaviour is partly accounted for by the debasement of human values caused by the extremity of war: 'the peer group can make people do *anything*, and do it day in and day out. In the rapist army, everybody raped. Even the colonels raped. And I raped too' (*HM* 27). This admission establishes a number of themes in the text. Firstly, that there is a particularly masculine idea behind the dehumanization of war and the victims are predominantly, although not only of course, women. As with *Yellow Dog*, Amis's exploration of the darker side of humanity is predominantly an exploration of masculine violence, both to other men and to women. The narrator's claims of love for Zoya are undercut by the last encounter the two characters have, when he rapes her after she has come to visit him in a very drunken state. In the letter from Lev that he reads towards the end of his life, we get the first external perspective on the narrator: 'It's very simple, you're violent' and this violence manifests itself in sexual acts of violence against women (*HM* 187).

One of the problematic aspects of Amis's fiction is his propensity to generalize about ethnic, racial and national characteristics. This can be seen regarding black and Asian characters in *Money, London Fields* and *The Information*, and as we saw in Chapter 5, the discussion of an essentialist German ethnicity in *Time's Arrow*. *House of Meetings* makes similar generalizations about the perceived Russian character.[16] The overriding image of Russia and Russianness provided by the narrator is one of a violent nature that in its extreme tends towards self-destruction. This reading of the Russian character exceeds Soviet or communist ideologies, and is identified in a much longer tradition of Russian history.[17] But again the place of the narrator is ambiguous here. He is clearly aware that his pronouncements of national and ethnic characteristics are generalizations bordering on stereotypes, but that these kinds of generalizations are part of the Eastern psyche, in contrast with his reading of the '*mild ideology* [that] *Nobody's going to blow themselves to bits for*' produced in the West, and which in his view claims to resist generalizations in subservience to relativistic individualism (*HM* 2). In one of the passages that offers a direct address to Venus he writes:

> Your crowd, they're so terrorstricken by generalisations that they can't even manage a declarative sentence [. . .] A generalisation might sound like an attempt to stereotype – and we can't have that. I'm at the other end. I worship generalisations. And the more sweeping the better. I am ready to kill for sweeping generalisations.
>
> The name of your ideology, in case anyone asks, is Westernism. It would be no use to you here. (*HM* 50)

The power of the narrator's argument is seductive here, but really it turns on a circularity that emphasizes that there is something intrinsically Eastern about using generalizations, and therefore the narrator's generalizations about Russian identity are valid in the context in which he is making them. The narrator also brings in essentializing arguments to support his reading of national character, especially in the terms of geography and the state, and the need for Russian leaders of whatever political hue to have an iron-firm hand over the populace: 'the Russian state, with its compulsive and self-protective expansion, its land empire of twenty nations, its continent-sized borders: all this demands a heavily authoritarian centre, a vast and vigilant bureaucracy – or else Russia flies apart [...] Geography did it' (*HM* 53). These arguments tend to fix Russianness at some point beyond discrete political systems ('I don't like Soviet power, and I don't like the tsars' (*HM* 12)).

Somewhat paradoxically, however, Lev's resistance to the dehumanizing effects of what appear to be the Russian norm contradicts the narrator's generalizations, as he too, of course, is part of that ethnic group. The reader is persuaded to reject some of the more outspoken generalizations about the Russian 'character' delivered by the narrator. Again, however, Amis is not in the business of providing easy moral frameworks for the reader in terms of characters and plot, but rather turns these moral dilemmas back onto the reader. To borrow from Roland Barthes's description of the difference between readerly and writerly texts, then, Amis's novels can be said to be the latter at the level of the moral, ethical and political.[18]

What is less ambiguous is the novel's emphasis on the effect of the camps to strip away any sense of human feeling (and ultimately conscience) in the face of absolute state power. The narrative emphasizes that 'the conscience, I suspect, is a vital organ. And when it goes, you go' (*HM* 171). This is the narrator's reasoning for the collapse of the Soviet Union in the 1990s, the fact that once a nation's conscience has been irreparably damaged, then the desire to reproduce is lost. Lev's letter sums up this position as the loss of the sense of play, as represented in the pleasure and freedom of sexual relationships. This is the central message revealed in Lev's letter about his experiences with Zoya in the house of meetings. As noted earlier, this was the name given to the isolated chalet where prisoners were allowed to spend time with their wives when some of the more stringent rules of the camps had been relaxed. This meeting is presented as a shadow over the whole of the text containing the vital insight into what it is that the state has destroyed in the human through its extreme coercive measures. In the letter, Lev explains that due to the crushing weight of the state on the individual any emotional pleasure is destroyed, so that sex becomes simply a physical act. This understanding is reached by Lev as he is having sex with Zoya, when he realizes that although his physical desire for his wife is undiminished by his time in the camps, his emotional response has been eroded. In the letter he describes how during sex all he could think about was, firstly, eating and, secondly, sleeping, ultimately reflecting that 'I had lost all my play. All' (*HM* 181).[19] Significantly, Lev, a poet before being placed in the camp, is unable to write poetry after this revelation in the chalet, a situation reminiscent of Theodore Adorno's famous statement that 'to write poetry after Auschwitz is barbaric'.[20] Poetry is allied to the human sensibilities, and once the joy of play has been removed by the state, then imaginative artistic production becomes futile. Similarly the desire to reproduce also becomes futile. As the narrator describes it in the final, italicized, part of the text: '*We will work for you, but we're not going to fuck for you any more. We are not going to go on doing it, making people. Making people to be set before the indifference of the state*' (*HM* 192). This imposition of the state over the joyful pleasure of sex is at the heart of the demise of the USSR according to the novel, although it takes several decades for this to be made manifest in the national psyche. The impact of this removal of playfulness is presented statistically in the trope of the two lines of the graph that shows the birth rate and death rate in Russia. The lines on this graph are seen to cross at some point in 1992, and are described poignantly by the narrator as the 'Russian cross' (*HM* 168). The idea of crossing over is also pursued when individuals reach a crucial (cruxial) turning-point in the victory of the state over their humanity.

The dehumanizing cruelty of the gulag is emphasized in the repeated use of animalistic terminology to describe its inmates. The groupings that reflect the hierarchical power structures include the pigs, the brutes and bitches, the snakes, the leeches, and the locusts. Amis also draws on a model of the regressive degeneration of human evolution, especially in the figure of Uglik, a character who takes on especial emblematic significance for the effects of gulag power over the individual. Uglik is described as an example of 'the emergence of human beings of a new type' (*HM* 88); and later that he 'came from the future' (*HM* 93). Uglik inflicts a physical blow on Lev that results in deafness in one ear, but the psychological effect on Lev is more profound. Uglik, after a bout of violence and drunkenness sleeps outside in subzero temperatures and as a consequence loses both his hands. The image of him later trying to light a cigarette becomes seared on Lev's imagination and becomes emblematic of the debasement of human nature: 'This was our master: the man scared so stupid that he kept forgetting he had no hands' (*HM* 96). As with *Yellow Dog*, Amis also uses canine imagery to indicate the debasement of human ethics. One powerful representation of this is in the description of the 'wild dogs' of Predposylov, who he sees on a return visit to the town where one of his camps was located and who appear to be the offspring of the dogs that roamed the camp in the 1950s. One of the powerful ironies of these 'wild' dogs, however, is the fact that they appear to be very disciplined, almost self-trained to be vicious. This produces a powerful analogy for the totalitarian state: 'The wild dogs of Predposylov don't look wild to me. They look trained – not by a human, but by another dog; and this superdog taught them all they knew' (*HM* 166).

7

Cast of Crooks[1]: *The Pregnant Widow* and *Lionel Asbo*

> 'How will it go, he often wondered, when all the brain-dead awaken?' (*LA* 166)

Amis's latest two novels to date have seen him garner more controversy, to the extent that it is now evident that baiting the literary reviewers may be part of the nature of his fiction, creating a sense of expectation, undoubtedly boosting sales, and to a certain extent affecting the way in which his fiction is understood. *The Pregnant Widow* offended on two counts: firstly in its portrayal of the shifting mores of sexuality in the wake of the sexual revolution; and secondly in its anticipation of a new cultural politics of ageing in terms of a 'silver-tsunami' and the age war.[2] *Lionel Asbo* shifted the critics' wrath to castigating what was seen to be Amis's contribution to the trend in twenty-first century culture of demonizing the white working class in Britain.

THE PREGNANT WIDOW

Amis's 2010 novel sees him returning to the terrain of *The Rachel Papers*. *The Pregnant Widow* follows the experience of a young man trying to fathom out his sexual attraction to women within the shifting mores of the period following the so-called sexual revolution of the 1960s. What is different in this novel is that you also get the long, backward view, supplied in short intervals from the perspective of the same character, now aged fifty, as he comes to terms with the effects ageing has on his appearance, body and outlook. The majority of the novel takes place in Italy in 1970 and is focalized through Keith Nearing, a 20-year-old English literature student holidaying in Italy with his girlfriend, Lily. They have been invited to stay for the summer at the family home of their friend Scheherazade, and the holiday sees them encountering a number of their other friends and acquaintances, both new and old. The action centres on Keith's growing attraction and possible affair with Scheherazade. Inevitably perhaps, the novel also details the decline of Keith's relationship with Lily. Hovering over this plotline is Amis's interest in mapping the effects on individuals of the sexual revolution and what he sees as some of the negative aspects of second-wave feminism.

The chapters set in 1970 form the major part of the novel, but these are interspersed with short passages that concern Keith in older life contemplating the effects of ageing, and there is a coda to the novel that fills in what happens to a number of the characters from 1970 to 2009. One of the more successful aspects of the novel is its account of the processes of ageing which stands in stark contrast to the youth presented in the main sections of the novel: 'As you pass the half-century, the flesh, the coating on the person, begins to attenuate. And the world is full of blades and spikes [. . .] Then you learn to protect yourself. This is what you'll go on doing until, near the end, you are doing nothing else – just protecting yourself' (*PW* 62–3). This account is delivered with the usual Amis irony: 'Old age wasn't for old people. To cope with old age, you really needed to be young – young, strong, and in peak condition' (*PW* 169). It is also apparent that Amis cannot avoid being controversial, even in this context, as he anticipates a new cultural war that stands in contrast to the gender war he observes in the 1970 section of the novel:

> There used to be the class system, and the race system, and the sex system. The three systems are gone or going. And now we have the age system [. . .] *Governance, for at least a generation,* Keith read, *will be a matter of transferring wealth from the young to the old.* And they won't like that, the young. They won't like the *silver tsunami,* with the old hogging the social services and stinking up the clinics and the hospitals, like an inundation of monstrous immigrants. There will be age wars, and chronological cleansing . . . (*PW* 230)

Ageing, however, is a minor theme of the novel and the controversy Amis's comments caused in this context were overshadowed by the novel's engagement with and misguided conflation of the sexual revolution with second-wave feminism.[3] Amis has claimed in an interview that he has been a feminist since the 1980s, however *The Pregnant Widow* problematizes that view through its objectification of women and a stereotypical focus on the female body engendered through a gaze that is decidedly male.[4] A chapter entitled 'Body Parts' focuses on the atomization of people into distinct physical items: for the observation of women, it tends to be breasts and buttocks, for men cocks and height. Particular relish is spent on discussions about Gloria Beautyman's 'arse' and Scheherazade's breasts. It could be argued that the narrative is focalized through Keith, and that this objectification is authentic for a young man growing up in the early 1970s; however, the narrative voice does not challenge Keith's perspective and the decision to use third-person narration in the novel tends to reinforce its deployment of dominant pre-second-wave-feminist gender codes. This objectification starts early, as can be seen in the way the three main characters in the first half of the novel are described by the third-person narrator: '34-25-34 (Lily), 37-23-33 (Scheherazade) – and Keith' (*PW* 8). This use of the 1970s habit of describing women in terms of their 'vital statistics' is partly parodied, but nevertheless it is a form of description Amis utilizes as a way to re-objectify the female characters. It is within the dominant cultural context of sexual inequalities that the novel engages with discourses of the sexual revolution. The main events of the novel in 1970 suggest that the drama will take place *in medias res* of the sexual revolution and the first main chapter begins with reference to Larkin's 'Annus Mirabilis' ('Sexual intercourse began / In 1963') but responds to the poem by suggesting that 'time had not yet trampled them flat [. . .] But now it was the summer of 1970, and sexual intercourse [. . .] had come a long way' (*PW* 7).

The main action, therefore, takes place within the process of the sexual revolution particularized in the range of sexual triangles and quadrangles the novel dramatizes.[5] As the narrator notes: 'Something was churning in the world of men and women, a revolution or a sea change, a realignment having to do with carnal knowledge and emotion' (*PW* 25). Amis's title refers to this sense of profound cultural and social transition; a new world has been engendered while older masculinities have died, leaving a feminized world without traditional patriarchy: 'And the old order gives way to the new, not immediately, though, not yet: the filled breasts and weakened knees, the cravings, the broken waters, the pumping womb, and labour, labour, labour' (*PW* 208). The text's reception of this imminent new world is ambivalent. In many ways the novel celebrates the newer loosening of restrictions on sexuality, but it also injects a note of caution, suggesting, from a position of hindsight, that the freedoms the sexual revolution unleashes will result in a number of predominantly female casualties.[6] 'It was already obvious that every hard and demanding adaptation would be falling to the girls. Not to the boys – who were all like that anyway. The boys could just go on being boys. It was the girls who had to choose. And ingenuousness was probably over. Maybe, in this new age, girls needed designs' (*PW* 371). The suggestion here is that the sexual revolution, as envisaged in some feminist discourse, lacked the adequate matriarchal templates. This lacuna in social genealogy for women results, in the novel's view, in some women adapting to the changes in sexual mores by taking on attributes of aggressive sexual promiscuity conventionally associated with patriarchal masculinity; as the narrator notes: 'girls acting like boys was in the air' (*PW* 24). This presumes, of course, that Amis or his characters (or both), are unaware of the long history of feminism (first and second wave) and its engagement with sexual politics.

Despite this lack of knowledge, the novel pursues a narrative that emphasizes the female victims of this unshackling of sexual behaviour from the inherited gender codes of the previous generation. The main victims are Gloria Beautyman and Keith's sister Violet, both of whom are punished in the novel by uncritically taking on those forms of predatory sexuality conventionally restricted to men. Violet is the most exaggerated character in this context, although she only appears in the novel in discussions others have about her, in particular those between Keith and his brother Kenrick.[7] In one such discussion, the reversal of conventional gender codes is apparent: 'You know the way you and me go on about chicks? That's the way she goes on about *guys* – guys she's fucked. Guy's don't fuck her. She fucks them' (*PW* 213). What is apparent here is the surprise Kenrick registers regarding Violet's approaches to relationships and what he is surprised about is the way in which Violet appears to have appropriated traditional masculine approaches to sexuality. This could be seen as a recognition of the way in which feminism was beginning to make an impact on gender relations, however Violet's fate in the novel undercuts any support for an emerging feminist politics focused on attaining gender equality in matters of sexual behaviour. In the coda we learn of Violet's rapid descent into increasing use of alcohol and other drugs as she continues to satisfy her large sexual appetite. Amis has included several male characters whose similar demise is to be lamented, but the way in which Violet's experience is reported second hand distances her particular situation, and results in a critique of the process by which the loosening of gender codes can have devastating effects on women. It can be argued that Violet's fate is more to do with her excessive character than the fact that her trajectory appears to critique some of the practical applications of feminist ideas. The character of Gloria Beautyman, however, offers an alternative critique. As with Violet, Gloria is provided with a rapacious sexual desire, but one that is articulated through a character given rational justifications for her approach to relationships. Gloria is described, and indeed describes herself, as a 'cock', indicating that she takes an active role in pursuing sex. That the active sexual role is designated in masculine terms is something to which I will return; however, the way she approaches relationships is clearly presented as mirroring traditional pre-sexual revolution, male behaviour. The way in which the relationships play out in the Italian section of the novel reflects this sexual framework. Keith is on the point of achieving his fantasy of sleeping with Scheherazade, when he unintentionally offends her by drunkenly attacking her religious beliefs. From this moment on, it is Gloria who emerges as the character with whom Keith is destined to have a relationship, and it is clear that she represents an alternative release for his sexual frustrations. Given this scenario, it is with some surprise that in the coda we learn that Keith and Gloria subsequently marry after a series of failures in the latter's attempt to find a rich husband. Eventually, however, Gloria's overturning of the conventional gendered sex codes results in her demise. It is more prolonged than with Violet, but what the novel presents us with is a socio-moral framework in which those women that appear to have embraced the sexual (and feminist) revolution ultimately suffer. Maybe this is because the society in which they are placed is not yet ready for such a sea change in gendered relations, although it seems to imply that the blame lies as much with the feminist discourses implicitly driving their behaviour as with the lingering patriarchal society against which they are judged.

In contrast with Violet and Gloria, Scheherazade's sexual experiences are more balanced and produce a more beneficial outcome. However, this is because she is unwilling to throw herself into the new promiscuity; as the narrator notes: 'Scheherazade, you belong to the old regime' (*PW* 335). Despite this appearing at first to be a criticism of Scheherazade for not being open enough to the new sexual mores, the plot of the novel cannot help congratulating her for her resistance to the cultural imperatives of the sexual revolution. In the coda we learn that she is one of the few characters who emerge from the 1970s relatively intact emotionally, and it is apparent that the reason for this is her restraint, and what might be seen as adhering to the older, patriarchal systems.

Despite Amis's claim to be a feminist, then, it is difficult not to see the architecture of the novel falling in line with older systems of gender coding, whereby aggressive and sexually promiscuous female characters are punished because of their behaviour. The idea of policing female sexuality is certainly complicated, but the novel does not escape the patriarchal conventions it claims to exceed. In one sense the novel shows that language itself at this period in time has not developed sufficiently to reveal any utopian ideal of gender equality. That Gloria Beautyman can only articulate her aggressive sexual drive in terms of the male member shows something of the paradoxes language establishes in this context. The novel, however, does not interrogate these socio-linguistic paradoxes sufficiently for the claim that it is feminist to be maintained.

As in most of Amis's novels, the way in which fiction and reality interconnect is a prominent feature of *The Pregnant*

Widow; as the narrator says 'the world is a book we can't put down' (*PW* 3).[8] However, the metafiction is much less pronounced than in *Other People*, *Money* or *London Fields*. Keith is an English literature student and the intertextual references in the text represent the books he is reading and so reflect the way he views the world through his literary imagination. They also serve as an indication of class difference:

> Keith was assuming that social realism would hold, here in Italy. And yet Italy itself seemed partly fabulous [. . .] Where was social realism? The upper classes themselves, he kept thinking, were not social realists. Their modus operandi, their way of operating, obeyed looser rules. He was, ominously, a K in a castle. But he was still assuming that social realism would hold. (*PW* 27–8)

Amis here identifies social class in terms of literary modes and clearly Keith and Lily ('the only novel she unreservedly praised was *Middlemarch*' (*PW* 27)) are part of the middle classes. The fact that Keith associates himself with the modernist hero of Kafka's *The Castle* suggests that the events on the holiday may potentially exceed Keith's usually quotidian experience.

The literary references also operate in the novel to track changes in the relationships between men and women historically, suggesting that *The Pregnant Widow* will attempt to place itself within this literary history of sexual relations.[9] Keith often ponders his present situation with respect to plots of the classic English novels he is reading, and the chronological way he moves from Austen to *Vanity Fair* and *Dracula*, Hardy and Lawrence, parallels the plot development in the scenes set in the castle. For example, he compares the situation between Emma and Mr Knightley in Austen's novel with his relationship with Scheherazade:

> If Keith paraphrased Mr Knightley, would Scheherazade realise, at last, that she was in love with him? No, because things were different now. And what had changed? Well, Emma's colloquy with Miss Bates, on Box Hill, was not about busts and backsides and (by implication) a day of shame at a sex tycoon's; and as she girded herself for censure, Emma didn't face Mr Knightley topless; and Gloria was not, or not yet, a spinster. All that, and this. In 1970, you could no longer love subliminally: the conscious mind worked full-time on love or what used to be love. (*PW* 198)

In Keith's comparison between past fiction and the present situation he begins to recognize two things. Firstly, that the parameters of social and sexual interaction have shifted and are continuing to shift during the period in which he finds himself; and secondly, that the literature of the past can no longer act as a weather-vane for guiding you through the present. The passage above marks the shift from love to sex as the driving force for relationships, and although it appears that discussion about sex is more open, it does not follow that that makes navigating relationships any easier. In this sense the novel represents a post-feminist reflection on the effects of the sexual revolution. This includes a reassessment of the ways in which sexuality can be read in novels of the past, such as Gloria Beautyman's reading of Elizabeth Bennett as a 'cock' (*PW* 315–21).

In conclusion, we might ask whether the novel succeeds in mapping the effects of the rapid changes in sexual mores during the period. Partly; but this judgement is qualified by the failure of the novel to escape from the very gendered language and outlooks it presents as part of the old world from which the new is trying to emerge. The way in which the novel identifies victims and survivors of the sexual revolution is in danger of being read as lamenting the very idea of a sexual revolution, which perhaps makes Amis closer to Larkin than he would like to admit. Amis's claim that the novel reflects his position as a feminist is much harder to justify given its reproduction of gendered forms of language and outlook, and perhaps it can be described as feminist only in the sense that it recognizes the way in which, in some circumstances, the attempt by women to appropriate dominant (stereotypical) codes of masculinity can be detrimental. The problem is that the novel seems to take comedic pleasure in the traditional sexist images of women, and the ironic distance with which we are encouraged to view Keith's ideas is ambivalent. In his defence, Amis is likely to argue that the job of the novel is to record in imaginative ways the experience of a generation, rather than offer a sociological discourse on the causes and effects of various social and cultural movements. Nevertheless, that does not exclude fiction from implicitly (and often explicitly) advocating a position in cultural politics. It is in this sense that Amis's next novel also caused a great deal of controversy with early reviewers and commentators: namely the political and ideological implications revealed in the aesthetic space generated between realistic depiction and imaginative construction.

LIONEL ASBO: STATE OF ENGLAND (2012)

Amis's thirteenth novel, *Lionel Asbo*, returns somewhat to the territory of *Yellow Dog* in its exploration of criminality and masculine violence in a contemporary urban, English setting.[10] The novel recounts the relationship between white, working-class Lionel, a violent criminal in his early twenties, and his 'mixed-race' nephew Des Pepperdine. Lionel has acted as a surrogate father to his nephew since the death of Des's mother Cilla (Lionel's sister). Lionel's role as a father figure, however, is compromised by the mixture of aggression and advice he supplies. At one point he chastises Des for watching *Crimewatch* making it very clear where he thinks Des should stand in relation to his own battle with the forces of law and order.[11] Des begins to recognize problems in this relationship earlier on, referring to Lionel as a kind of anti-dad, but it is clear that he has a deep familial bond with his wayward uncle. This family relationship is complicated by the fact that when the novel opens we learn that Des has recently been having an affair with his grandmother (and Lionel's mother) Grace, Des being just fifteen at the time. As this opening shows, Amis is again keen to grab the attention of his readers through a morally provocative scenario and it is somewhat surprising that Des emerges as the most sympathetic character in the novel, though perhaps given the nature of the eponymous anti-hero, it is not surprising that, by contrast, Des holds the moral centre. Lionel's surname was also once Pepperdine, but we learn that he has changed it by deed poll to Asbo, to reflect the pride he takes in his aggressive and anti-social track record. He is registered as the youngest person to receive an Anti-Social Behaviour Order at the age of three because of his terrorizing of Diston, the fictional east London council estate on which he was brought up. This start in life sets the tone for his adulthood: when the novel opens Lionel works on the shadier side of debt collection and as a career criminal is 'almost up to PhD level on questions of criminal law. Criminal law, after all, was the third element in his vocational trinity, the other two being villainy and prison' (*LA* 17). It is presented, therefore, as an unfair twist of serendipity when Lionel, whilst on one of his periods in prison, wins several millions on the lottery, a fact the prison governor suggests 'proves that God's got a sense of humour' (*LA* 81).

As is usual with the arrival of a new Amis novel, the reviews of *Lionel Asbo* were mixed and centred on whether Lionel (and to a lesser extent Des) represents an accurate portrayal of contemporary working-class (or under-class) culture, and what right Amis had, as a member of a privileged, upper-middle-class social sphere, to describe the lives of those people living on urban council estates.[12] Many attacked it for its stereotyping of working-class culture, and in particular its relevance to the vogue concept in twenty-first century Britain of so-called chav culture. The mis-representation of working-class culture is an area that the critic and commentator Owen Jones has written on in his book *Chavs: The Demonization of the Working Class*, which was published the year before *Lionel Asbo*. As Jones writes:

> Chav-bashing has become a way of making money because it strikes a chord [...] this form of class hatred has become an integral, respectable part of Modern British culture. It is present in newspapers, TV comedy shows, films, internet forums, social networking sites and everyday conversations. At the heart of the 'chavs' phenomenon is an attempt to obscure the reality of the working-class majority.[13]

There are elements of Amis's fiction in which Jones's critique holds weight, especially in the representation of Diston – the fictional east London council estate where most of the action of the novel takes place. However, it is clear that Lionel is not representative of working-class culture in the way Jones's criticism suggests, but an exaggerated metaphorical symptom of a nation which allows and even promotes the kind of behaviour and ethos to which he subscribes. In this sense the target is not the class from which he emerges but the ideologies pertaining within Britain that can produce a figure such as Lionel Asbo. The 'state of England' subtitle alerts the reader to the way in which the character is to be seen as representative of current socio-political conditions, conditions that are in part producing Lionel's rationalization of his social position. Lionel's intelligence often comes into question but, as Des identifies, he is clearly not stupid and his career criminality is based on a rational philosophy developed with respect to the limited options society offers him. The novel, therefore, addresses the hoary old question of how far criminal behaviour can be justified in a society in which individuals, due to their social and political circumstances, are engaged in breaking the laws of a system that is designed to exploit the class to which they belong. If this sounds like a Marxist reading of the novel, then indeed there is a lingering Marxist critique in much of Amis's assessment of contemporary British society, even if he would reject Marxist solutions. The limited educational opportunities available to Lionel are made clear in the description of Squeers Free School, which, 'set the standard for the most police call-outs, the least GCSE passes, and the highest truancy rates' (LA 19). Lionel's period at Squeers had it seems inevitably led to him being 'offrolled' to a Young Offender Institution, which he, 'always spoke of [...] with rueful fondness, like one recalling a rite of passage' (*LA* 19).

As with *Yellow Dog*, the Fourth Estate is a key target of the way in which figures like Lionel Asbo are manipulated and reproduced, and the slippage between realism and the tabloid construction of his world is crucial in this context. Des's narrative of growing self-awareness and advancement has a key first stage in identifying the nature of the ideological effects of the darker side of tabloid journalism: when first encountering a range of newspapers in the library we learn: 'Until now he [Des] had accepted the *Morning Lark* as an accurate reflection of reality. Indeed he sometimes thought it was a local paper [...] Now, though, as he stood there with the *Sun* quivering in his hands, the *Lark* stood revealed for what it was – a daily lads' mag, perfunctorily posing as a journal of record' (*LA* 21). In many ways, Lionel is the kind of mediatized and demonized figure of the underclass that appears in the tabloid press. As Des notes, once Lionel becomes famous, he, 'disappear[s] into the front page' (*LA* 101). Many of the early reviewers who recognized this fact, however, failed to go on to identify the way in which the novel begins to complicate that media construction.

That the novel engages with contemporary English society in a non-realist context of grotesques was announced by the cover of the first edition, which carries a cartoon image of Lionel by David Hughes, suggesting that the eponymous character within its pages should also be treated as cartoonish.[14] It is clear that Lionel Asbo is not meant to be representative of the working class generally, but of an exaggerated, and largely media-constructed image. The nature of the cartoon as a form is that it is two-dimensional, but Lionel begins to be given depth in the sections that detail the growth of self-awareness and an inner voice, which could be read as the development of a social conscience: 'He was having a conversation with what seemed to be a higher intelligence. The voice was cleverer than he was' (*LA* 117). As Lionel begins to develop this other dimension the reader's sympathies gradually warm to him to a certain extent, and we begin to see him as a dupe and a sacrificial lamb set upon the ideological altar of the media.[15] The two-dimensional aspect of his personality is thus presented as a representation of the way in which individuals like Lionel are constructed by the tabloid press, represented in the novel by the *Morning Lark*. In a literary mode of this kind, little mileage is gained is assessing the accuracy of the portrayal against 'authentic' social models in the real world.[16]

Where the novel can, however, be accused of generalization in class terms is in its depiction of the council estate on which the Pepperdines live before Lionel wins the lottery. Diston is described as 'a world of italics and exclamation marks' (*LA* 34), in which 'everything hated everything else, and everything else, in return, hated everything back' (*LA* 165). It is an area in which procreation starts early and people rarely live beyond fifty. This kind of stereotyping exceeds the singularity of a figure such as Lionel and serves to reinforce tired and patronizing representations of urban sink estates. However, the comic exaggeration with which Amis treats Diston is similarly contrasted with Short Crendon – the wealthy English village to which Lionel moves after his lottery win, where, 'everything contemplated everything else with unqualified satisfaction' (*LA* 165). As we have seen in several of Amis's novels, when the fiction relies on stock generalizations about cultural identities it loses some of its impact as a serious commentary on existing social conditions.

However, here there is a clear attempt at identifying the widening gap between rich and poor in early twenty-first-century Britain, and to identify 'two nations' or, perhaps, to evoke C. P. Snow's phrase from a different context, 'two cultures' within England. Lionel's 'fairy tale' narrative is effectively the move between these two cultures. As Lionel tells Daphne, a reporter from *The Sun*: 'the rich world...is heavy. Everything weighs [...] And *my* old world, Diston as was, it's...it's light! Nothing weighs an ounce! People die! [...] So that's me challenge. To go from the floating world...to the heavy' (*LA* 151). This transition proves difficult for Lionel and we get the sense that his heart is never really in it. When Lionel first enters the world of the rich he suffers an existential crisis, brought on by moving between the two cultures: 'See, Des, there's something new in my life. A new uh, *dimension*. [...] The future!' (*LA* 105). He begins to feel out of place, and experiences a novel sense of embarrassment with his normal, aggressive behaviour. This comes to a head with the scene in an expensive Knightsbridge restaurant, in which Lionel dines alone, dressed up in a manner that one of the paparazzi jokes makes him look like a bingo caller. After an exchange with Cuthburt, the fawning restaurant owner, he ruins his expensive shahtoosh suit in trying to get at the lobster meat he has ordered in its shell, and inadvertently reveals the pornographic pages of the *Morning Lark* to a shocked upper-class clientele. The embarrassment this series of incidents causes is a new feeling for Lionel and the culture shock proves ultimately to be too much for him. After leaving the restaurant he purposely gets himself put back in prison by beating up several members of the press when he is fully aware that there is a 'copper watching' (*LA* 128). That Lionel feels more comfortable in prison is reminiscent of Camus's epigram about the freedom of the condemned man, or as Lionel puts it: 'when you in prison, you have you peace of mind. Because you not worried about getting arrested' (*LA* 269–70).

In fact, it is not Lionel's criminality that is the main target for the novel's satire, but the brand of celebrity culture that Amis feels has developed in Britain over the last twenty years or so. Celebrity is identified by two main types in the text: firstly, those popular cultural icons who enhance their public visibility through (largely masculine) anti-social behaviour; and secondly, those who pursue celebrity for its own sake. The former are presented in the novel as being on a continuum with Lionel's outlook on life:

> He made several good mates during his short time there [the South Central Hotel]. Scott Ronson, the arthritic, lantern-jawed rhythm guitarist of a band called the Pretty Faces. Eamon O'Nolan, the two-time World Snooker Champion (who was always doing community service for various unambitious misdemeanours – roughing up referees, relieving himself in pot plants, and the like). Lorne Brown, the winner of a huge reality telethon (a month in the South Central was one of his prizes). Brent Medwin, the (teenage) cokehead Manchester City midfielder, both of whose parents were in jail (the mum for living off immoral earnings, the dad for manslaughter). Hereabouts, Lionel Asbo could just relax and be himself, freely mingling with his fellow superstars. (*LA* 113)

The second kind is represented by 'Threnody', an aspiring female celebrity, who seeks out Lionel after his lottery win; she insists on having her name in quotation marks, suggesting that she only really exists as a constructed media image. 'Threnody' represents what the novel sees as the kind of modern celebrity for whom fame is the driving ambition and whose life (and body) becomes wholly a performance. It is not that the novel suggests that the type she represents is talentless, rather that her talent *is* the pursuit of celebrity status. Her success in turning Lionel into a '*national treasure*' (*LA* 113) is part of her own celebrity agenda once they are romantically attached and her constant battle with the more successful Danube, her arch rival in the same celebrity field, marks out the key motivational feature of all her behaviour. Lionel, however, is unable or unwilling to be 'celebrified' in the way 'Threnody' wishes; as he complains to Des after one publicity event she organizes: 'What's happening Des? Me face – me face, Des, it's all distorted! From the *smiling*. I can't get it back to what it was before! What's happening? Where's Lionel Asbo? Gone. I'm gone, boy, I'm gone' (*LA* 181).

In a BBC interview Amis gave on the release of *Lionel Asbo* he cited its aim, as ever with his fiction, as being to educate and entertain.[17] The novel entertains at the comic level, partly through the cartoonish figure of Asbo and partly through its style. Two main stylistic techniques are deployed. Firstly, there is a style that could be called inverted free indirect discourse, in which the narrator presents characters in language from a register associated with a distinctly different social and cultural milieu to the one the characters inhabit. Asbo is most often presented in this way. The second technique is satirical exaggeration, which is used particularly in the second half of the novel to describe Lionel's behaviour once he becomes a celebrity. The aim to educate, however, is more problematic. The novel appears, in part, to be stressing sympathy with Lionel, blaming the causes for his behaviour on the abandonment and ghettoization of the underclass from which he springs. In this sense, it is difficult to disentangle who or what needs educating: Lionel, or the system that has produced him.

The 'State of England' subtitle makes it clear that the novel is partly a critique of contemporary British culture and the target is not Lionel Asbo but the culture that promotes and encourages his behaviour. It is not a critique of the welfare state but of the ideological forces that operate to contain the working classes, to make sure that their ambitions are not of the order to challenge conventional society. As Owen Jones implies, this novel might have been more effective had it been written by someone who had firsthand experience of the council estates – but it would probably have been a very different kind of novel. To restrict depictions of working-class life to social realism, which in fact is often romanticized and sentimental, is clearly a form of literary ghettoization. Cultural celebrity produces grotesques, and often it frames them in a way that popularizes some of the negative aspects of working-class culture. But Lionel Asbo is not representative of the working class, or even the underclass. He is a monstrous singularity created not by Amis alone, but by a media culture that serves to demonize the working class. Lionel is a mirror, reflecting the way in which many in the middle classes in Britain would like to think of working-class culture. Amis is not part of the problem, as many of the critics seemed to suggest, but is identifying the malady in the cultural frameworks pertaining in Britain with respect to the representation of working-class people and culture generally. In this sense, I think the spirit of Jones's critique is good, but his reading of the novel has missed some of the complexities of Amis's form of cultural representation; and indeed both are closer than at first appears in their view of the cultural politics of contemporary representations of white working-class culture.

The responsibility is not solely down to cultural and ideological forces, as can be seen in Des's attempt to educate himself. A significant difference between Amis's novel and some of the other working-class novels of the post-1945 period such as John Wain's *Hurry on Down* and John Braine's *Room at the Top*, is that the trajectory of the novel is not out of the estate, and by implication out of the culture, but to ameliorate the culture from within. At the end of the novel Des, his wife Dawn, and their new baby daughter Cilla are settling down to build a warm, loving family on the estate. Des works for *The Daily Mirror* as a reporter, which is perhaps not identified as a conventional working-class occupation; however, it is within that lower-middle, upper-working class that the novel places cultural value – a tradition of education and intellectual thought, that chimes with many Left-leaning intellectuals in the post-war period. The decision to not have Des and Dawn leave the estate is crucial in a novel that carries the subtitle 'State of England'. The implication is that the council estates should not be abandoned and should not be overtaken by the more media-visible manifestations of working-class culture as represented in the cartoonish figure of Lionel.

Notes

INTRODUCTION

1. Amis corroborates this sentiment in an interview with Will Self when he says: 'In an age of growing literalism... there's also the vulgar interest in the writer himself – or herself. Because personalities are much more accessible than a corpus of work. Everyone can understand a person, you can see them on Terry Wogan, and you've got a handle on them. In TV age terms, it's pretty onerous to have to wade through a body of work, when all you're interested in is personalities.' Will Self, 'An Interview with Martin Amis', *Mississippi Review*, 3 Oct. 1993, 143–69.
2. See Amis, 'The American Eagle', *The War Against Cliché: Essay and Reviews 1971–2000* (London: Jonathan Cape, 2001), 467. For an excellent discussion of the relationship between style and morality in Amis's fiction, see David James, '"Style is Morality"? Aesthetics and Politics in the Amis Era', *Textual Practice*, 26/1 (2012), 11–25.
3. Adam Mars-Jones, 'Anti-Dad', *London Review of Books*, 21 June 2012.
4. George Eliot, 'The Natural History of German Life', in *The Essays of George Eliot*, ed. Thomas Pinney (New York: Princeton University Press, 1963), 266–99.
5. Raymond Williams, *Problems in Materialism and Culture* (London: Verso, 1980), 36–45.
6. Interview with Amis for the *Observer Review*, 8 Sept. 2002.

CHAPTER 1. AMIS AND FATHER: *THE RACHEL PAPERS* AND *EXPERIENCE*

1. In *Experience*, Amis notes that the review of *The Rachel Papers* by Peter Prince, 'saw no irony, no stylisation – no difference at all between me and my narrator' (*E* 34). See Peter Prince, 'Review of

Martin Amis, *The Rachel Papers*', *Times Literary Supplement*, 14 Nov. 1973.

2. James Diedrick, *Understanding Martin Amis*, 2nd edn (Columbia: University of South Carolina Press, [1995] 2004), 28–39.
3. I have written elsewhere on Kingsley Amis's association with the 'angry young men'. See 'Anger Management: Kingsley Amis and John Wain' in *Radical Fictions: The English Novel in the 1950s* (Oxford: Peter Lang, 2007), 127–56.
4. Kingsley Amis, *Lucky Jim* (Harmondsworth: Penguin, [1954] 1961).
5. See the parallel description in the letter from *Experience* in Amis's attempts to rehearse different character types to appeal to the Oxford entrance interviewer (*E* 108).
6. The other autobiographical book, *Koba the Dread: Laughter and the Twenty Million* is far more concerned with discussing Amis's view of the political naivety of many of his friends and acquaintances in their uncritical support for Marxism and Russian communism despite the knowledge of Stalin's atrocities. I discuss this book briefly in Chapter 6.
7. He takes up this pattern of an ironic distance of an older to a younger self in the two main time frames of Keith Nearing in *The Pregnant Widow*. See Chapter 7.
8. 'Interview with Martin Amis' in Margaret Reynolds and Jonathan Noakes, *Martin Amis: The Essential Guide* (London: Vintage, 2003), 12–26, 22.
9. Amis has stated in interview that it is in his 2010 novel *The Pregnant Widow* that he attempts to come to terms with his relationship with Sally. See interview with Mark Lawson for BBC Radio 4, *Front Row*, first broadcast 1 Feb. 2010.
10. Pat Kavanagh died in 2008.
11. Harold Bloom has argued that many writers have a Freudian relationship with their literary fathers, and the Amises represent an interesting example in this context, although it should be stressed that in *The Rachel Papers* a distinction should be made between the main character's relationship with his fictional father and the real-life relationship between Martin and Kingsley. As discussed in subsequent chapters, Amis draws heavily in his fiction from Freudian models of the psychosocial and psychosexual, Harold Bloom, *The Anxiety of Influence: A Theory of Poetry* (Oxford: Oxford University Press, 1973).
12. The morality of engaging with horrific real life in a fictional context is also an important aspect of *Time's Arrow*. It is significant that reviewers of both works commented on the moral implications of this kind of approach.
13. Richard Bradford, *Martin Amis: The Biography* (London: Constable,

2011). For Amis's criticism of the accuracy of this biography see the interview with Tom Lamont, 'Martin Amis: a New Chapter in America', *Observer*, 3 June 2012. Despite the claimed inaccuracies and the stylistic problems, Bradford's book offers an insight into Amis's background and experiences.

CHAPTER 2. CLASS ACTS: *DEAD BABIES* AND *SUCCESS*

1. James Diedrick, *Understanding Martin Amis*, 2nd edn (Columbia: University of South Carolina Press, [1995] 2004), 22.
2. Richard Todd, 'Looking-Glass Worlds in Martin Amis's Early Fiction: Reflectiveness, Mirror Narcissism, and Doubles', in Gavin Keulks (ed.), *Martin Amis: Postmodernism and Beyond* (Basingstoke: Palgrave Macmillan, 2006), 22–35.
3. Dominic Head makes a similar claim with respect to Amis's 1984 novel *Money: A Suicide Note*, which he describes as producing 'a new and vital form of satire [that] is also deeply (and knowingly) implicated in the effects of the ideology that it would repudiate', Dominic Head, *The State of the Novel: Britain and Beyond* (Malden, Mass. and Oxford: Blackwell-Wiley, 2008), 35.
4. *Dead Babies* was first published in 1975, although Amis was working on it from the end of the publication of his first novel *The Rachel Papers* in 1973.
5. Northrop Frye, *The Anatomy of Criticism: Four Essays* (Princeton and Oxford: Princeton University Press, [1957] 1971), 311.
6. Amis is clearly repelled by the name Keith. It reappears in several of his novels and is usually used to indicate a character of lower-middle or working-class origin who is repugnant in some way and usually morally defunct. See, for example, the character of Keith Talent in *London Fields*.
7. It is a type of comic exaggeration that Amis has used throughout his career returning with provocative force in his 2012 novel *Lionel Asbo*.
8. I refer here to the tradition of English realism, established in the nineteenth century, as a form that carries a moralistic agenda of extending the reader's sympathies to other people through access to the inner feelings and emotions of a fictional character. This tradition is most closely associated with George Eliot. See, in particular, her essay 'The Natural History of German Life', where she writes, 'The greatest benefit we owe to the artist, whether painter, poet, or novelist is the extension of our sympathies', George Eliot, 'The Natural History of German Life', in *The Essays of George Eliot*, ed. Thomas Pinney (New York: Princeton University

Press, 1963), 266–99, 270.

9. It is interesting to note that these characters are excluded from William Marsh's film adaptation of the novel *Dead Babies* (2000), directed by Marsh, Gruber Films.
10. Amis uses the technique of initially deploying a strict structural framework which then gradually breaks down in a number of his novels including *Success* (1978), *Money: A Suicide Note* (1984), *London Fields* (1989) and *Yellow Dog* (2003).
11. See Timothy Leary, Ralph Metzner and Richard Alpert, *The Psychedelic Experience: A Manual Based on the Tibetan Book of the Dead* (New York: Citadel Underground, [1964] 1995).
12. Although Marvell is perhaps not a direct parody of Leary, he is certainly based on the kind of individual influenced by Leary's philosophies in the mind-expanding and controlling possibilities of the use of psychedelic drugs. See n.11 above.
13. James Diedrick has noted this aspect of Amis's novel which he describes as a 'coruscating satire on countercultural narcissism [that] mandates a descent into moral atavism', James Diedrick, 'J. G. Ballard's "Inner Space" and the Early Fiction of Martin Amis', in Keulks (ed.), *Martin Amis: Postmodernism and Beyond*, 180–96, 186. Diedrick also makes a strong case for identifying the influence J. G. Ballard's work has on *Dead Babies*, in terms of theme and form, especially Ballard's *The Drowned World* and *Crash*.
14. Diedrick, *Understanding Martin Amis*, 43.
15. This onanistic theme is one that Amis returns to in the character of John Self in *Money: A Suicide Note.*
16. Mikhail Bakhtin, *Problems of Dostoevsky's Poetics*, trans. Caryl Emerson (Minneapolis: University of Minnesota Press, 1984), 115–16.
17. Diedrick cites Amis's presentation of 'those conversations' as one of the ways in which he engages with the Menippean tradition of satire (Diedrick, *Understanding Martin Amis*, 42).
18. Bakhtin, *Problems of Dostoevsky's Poetics*, 119.
19. Amis returns to a reappraisal of the impact of the 1960s cultural and sexual revolutions on individuals in his 2010 novel *The Pregnant Widow.*
20. Initially *Dead Babies* has a similar tight structure, but this begins to break down as the novel moves forward, a pattern Amis also uses in *London Fields.*
21. As will become apparent, Amis, like one of his main influences Dickens, often uses comic names to reflect aspects of a character's social standing, or physical and/or psychological characteristics.
22. For an incisive discussion of the link between style and morality in Amis's work see David James, '"Style is Morality"? Aesthetics and

Politics in the Amis Era', *Textual Practice*, 26/1 (2012), 11–25.
23. Diedrick, *Understanding Martin Amis*, 47.
24. Ibid. 54.

CHAPTER 3. METAFICTIONAL MYSTERIES: *OTHER PEOPLE* AND *MONEY*

1. The meaning and use of metafiction has been discussed by several critics including Mark Currie, *Postmodern Narrative Theory* (Basingstoke: Palgrave Macmillan, 1998); Linda Hutcheon, *A Poetics of Postmodernism: History, Theory, Fiction* (London and New York: Routledge, 1988); David Lodge, *The Modes of Modern Writing: Metaphor, Metonymy and the Typology of Modern Literature* (London: Edward Arnold, 1979); and Patricia Waugh, *Metafiction: The Theory and Practice of Self-Conscious Fiction* (London: Methuen & Co., 1984).
2. Amis is not alone during the period in focusing on these issues; several British writers came to prominence in the 1970s and 1980s who were grouped under the heading of postmodernists including A. S. Byatt, Angela Carter, Ian McEwan, Salman Rushdie and Emma Tennant, all of whom have used metafiction in their fiction.
3. In an interview with Mira Stout, Amis recalls his father's criticism of *Money* as 'buggering around with the reader' at the point when the character 'Martin Amis' enters the novel. See Mira Stout, 'Martin Amis: Down London's Mean Streets', *New York Times Book Review*, 4 Feb. 1990.
4. It is probably accurate to see British fiction as a decade or so behind American fiction in the context of postmodernism becoming a regular feature of writing, despite there being an early tradition of British writers experimenting with techniques that were later identified as postmodern, including Christine Brook-Rose, B. S. Johnson, John Fowles, and to a lesser extent, Doris Lessing and Muriel Spark.
5. Amis describes his politics at this period as 'libertarian left of centre' (*E* 191n.). When he was writing *Other People* he was Literary Editor of the left-wing *New Statesman*, and close friends with the then Trotskyists Christopher Hitchens and James Fenton. Amis would, therefore, have been well-versed in Marxist theory, if he did not exactly share the political beliefs of his friends and colleagues.
6. Although Amis rarely quotes Freud directly, he appears to endorse a reading of human psychology that emphasizes the importance of the unconscious in determining behaviour, especially in the writer. In *Experience*, he writes that novels are 'messages from your

unconscious history' (*E* 218n.), and, 'Your writing comes from the back of your mind, where thoughts are unformulated and anxiety is silent' (*E* 280).

7. Absolute except that she, perhaps unconvincingly, finds that she remembers how to read. Given the hyper-real situation of the novel it is perhaps churlish to criticize Amis for this inconsistency and poetic licence should be allowed here, as Mary being able to read is crucial for her being able to understand the alien world in which she finds herself.
8. James Diedrick, *Understanding Martin Amis,* 2nd edn (Columbia: University of South Carolina Press, [1995] 2004), 58–61. As Diedrick notes, 'Martian' is also an intriguing anagram of 'Martin A'. As well as Craig Raine, the poets using 'Martian' techniques include Christopher Reid, David Sweetman and Oliver Reynolds.
9. The primary emotional state of the 'other people' inhabiting this world is melancholy, and it is no coincidence that late in the novel Mary finds a photograph representing the figure of death in the pages of *The Anatomy of Melancholy* – Robert Burton's extended Renaissance treatise on the nature of melancholia in the human psyche (*OP* 197). Robert Burton, *The Anatomy of Melancholy* (Oxford: Oxford University Press, [1621] 1994).
10. He does not use a female character as the main narrator again until *Night Train* (1997).
11. As we shall see in Chapter 7, this is a theme to which Amis returns in *The Pregnant Widow.*
12. I refer here to Simone de Beauvoir, *The Second Sex*, ed. and trans. H. M. Parshley (London: Jonathan Cape, [1949] 1953).
13. Friedrich Nietzsche, *Thus Spoke Zarathustra,* trans. Adrian del Caro, ed. Robert Pippin (Cambridge: Cambridge University Press, [1896] 2006).
14. The French theorist Michel Foucault tends to see power operating in the world in terms of local situations and frameworks, rather than in the broader class-stratified ways more commonly associated with a Marxist understanding of power. See *Discipline and Punish* trans. Alan Sheridan (New York: Pantheon, 1977).
15. Richard Todd, 'Looking-Glass Worlds in Martin Amis's Early Fiction: Reflectiveness, Mirror Narcissism, and Doubles', in Gavin Keulks (ed.), *Martin Amis: Postmodernism and Beyond* (Basingstoke: Palgrave Macmillan, 2006), 22–35. Although Todd does not relate his reading directly to psychoanalysis, it is implicit in his use of terms such as the inverse mirror narcissism.
16. Jacques Lacan, *Ecrits: A Selection*, trans. Alan Sheridan (New York: Norton, 1977). For Lacan, the mirror stage involves the identification of the concept of the self, when a toddler recognizes itself in a

mirror for the first time. This recognition, however, is far from straightforward as the figure in the mirror appears to be a much more unified and capable version of the self. This mirror image contrasts with the baby's internal perception of itself as a number of disconnected components – hands, arms, feet, mouth, etc. – whilst the mirror image appears to be a unity and in control of its motor powers. The 'Ideal-I' observed in the mirror, as Lacan terms it, thus presents a more controlled version to which the inner self aspires.

17. This theme of replaying a past memory can also explain Amis's use of double quotation marks in the meeting between Mary/Amy and her sister 'Baby' towards the end of the novel. Typographically, the last words they say to each other are placed in two sets of quotation marks suggesting a previous meeting at which the same lines were uttered. The encounter, therefore, is itself a reiteration of the past and suggests both a double encounter and a double parting (*OP* 199).
18. James Diedrick, for one, describes *Money* as a highwater mark in Amis's career, Diedrick, *Understanding Martin Amis*, 73.
19. See ibid. 36.
20. Fred Botting, 'From Excess to the New World Order', in Nick Bentley (ed.), *British Fiction of the 1990s*, (London and New York: Routledge, 2005), 21–41, 23.
21. Amis has commented that the novel represents him maturing and rejecting the 'childishness' of his earlier self (*E* 177).
22. Joe Brooker has written a thoughtful piece on the implications of this passage of the novel in which he identifies Amis's deployment of a Derridean sense of irresponsibility rubbing up against the worrying and unsettling set pieces that emphasize John Self's excessive behaviour. Joseph Brooker, 'License is Given: *Money* and the Menace of Comedy', in *Critical Engagements: A Journal of Criticism and Theory*, 3/2 (2009), 73–92.
23. Diedrick, *Understanding Martin Amis*, 73. Amis can here be seen to be drawing on one of his main literary influences – Nabokov, who hones this technique in his 1955 novel *Lolita*.
24. This is reminiscent of an entry in one of Evelyn Waugh's notebooks about trying to convey the complexities of real people in the tradition of the British novel, which tends to prefer characters that have consistent world views. When describing a real acquaintance as a source for a character he writes: 'she is hateful and lovable, covetous and open-handed, cruel and kind, malicious and generous of spirit, egotistic and unselfish. How on earth is a novelist so to combine these incompatible traits as to make the plausible harmony that renders a character credible?', W. Somerset Maugham, *A Writer's Notebook* (London: Vintage, [1949] 2001), 174–5.

25. Amis refers to the two main British youth subcultures of the period as he sees them: the stegosaurus-haired rock/heavy metal fans; and the parrot-crested punks.
26. The term 'race riot' is a misnomer in this context. Although one of the grievances that led to the riots was the feeling amongst Black and Asian communities that they were unfairly treated by the police, the street violence included people from many backgrounds and ethnicities, including white and black youth in particular.
27. In *Other People*, Mary observes: 'Money had recently done something unforgiveable: no one seemed to be able to forgive money for what it had done' (*OP* 57). Money is shown to saturate the society in which Mary finds herself and is clearly a crucial factor in each of the social classes she encounters. In one of the explicatory passages supplied by Prince he explains with respect to her relationship with Jock and Trev, the criminal muggers she falls in with at the opening of the novel: 'It's all about money, of course, like so much else' (*OP* 40). However, the influence of money as a force determines the way in which characters cope with emotional and psychological crises, and money is shown to alleviate the suffering to a significant extent. As the wealthy Jamie notes: 'God, it's so lucky that we've got all this money. I mean, where would we *be* if I didn't have all this money?' (*OP* 181). This outlook is confirmed later by Mary, possibly because she has by this time achieved a state of comparability with the other fallen: 'Amy had a lot of time for money and thought people seriously undervalued it. Money was more versatile than people let on' (*OP* 193).
28. Amis's relationship with Marxism has been the source of much debate, as evidenced by the public spat he had with the Marxist literary critic Terry Eagleton in 2007. See Terry Eagleton, 'Rebuking obnoxious views is not just a personality kink', *Guardian*, 10 Oct. 2007; and *Ideology: An Introduction*, new ed. (London: Verso, 2007), x–xi. Amis was close friends with Christopher Hitchens and James Fenton during this period, who were both actively engaged in Marxist politics and ideas; all three of them worked at the *New Statesmen* in the 1970s.
29. For a discussion of the Anglo-American economic context in Amis's novel see Jon Begley, 'Satirizing the Carnival of Postmodern Capitalism: The Transatlantic and Dialogic Structure of Martin Amis's *Money*', *Contemporary Literature* 45/1 (2004), 79–105. Margaret Thatcher's 'There's no such thing as society' quotation appears in Douglas Keay, 'Aids Education and the Year 2000', in *Woman's Own*, 31 Oct. 1987, 8–10.
30. That Self is eventually duped by Fielding Goodney and Doris Arthur could also be read politically as the way in which Thatcher/

Reagan monetarism had duped the electorate.

31. Amis was at this time also involved in writing the screenplay for a Hollywood film, *Saturn 3*, starring Kirk Douglas, Farah Fawcett and Harvey Keitel.
32. See Leonard R. N. Ashley, '"Names Are Awfully Important": The Onomastics of Satirical Comment in Martin Amis's *Money: A Suicide Note*', *Literary Onomastics Studies* 14 (1987), 1–48.

CHAPTER 4. MILLENNIAL FICTIONS: *LONDON FIELDS* AND *TIME'S ARROW*

1. D. M. Thomas's *The White Hotel* garnered similar criticism for its apparent inappropriateness of form and content with respect to its engagement with the Holocaust.
2. I am following Linda Hutcheon's central thesis here as argued in her excellent book *The Politics of Postmodernism* (London: Routledge, 1989).
3. *London Fields* famously did not make the Booker Prize shortlist in 1989 because two members of the panel, Maggie Gee and Helen McNeil, objected to its sexism. Nicolas Treddell discusses this in *The Fiction of Martin Amis: A Reader's Guide to Essential Criticism* (Basingstoke: Palgrave Macmillan, 2000), 97–100. See also Sara Mills, 'Working with Sexism: What Can Feminist Text Analysis Do?' in *Twentieth-Century Fiction: From Text to Context* (London: Routledge, 1995), 206–19.
4. Susan Brook, 'The Female Form, Sublimation, and Nicola Six' in Gavin Keulks (ed.), *Martin Amis: Postmodernism and Beyond* (Basingstoke: Palgrave Macmillan, 2006), 87–100, 91.
5. See, for example, Susie Thomas, 'Posing as a Postmodernist: Race and Class in Martin Amis's *London Fields*', *Literary London Journal* 1/2 (Sept. 2003). Although I think Thomas's discussion of class in the novel misses the mark, I agree with her reading of race.
6. Pierre Bourdieu, *Distinction: A Social Critique of the Judgement of Taste*, trans. R. Nice (Cambridge, Mass.: Harvard University Press, 1984).
7. Philip Tew, 'Martin Amis and Late-twentieth-century, Working-class Masculinity: *Money* and *London Fields*', in Keulks (ed.) *Martin Amis: Postmodernism and Beyond*), 71–86, 81.
8. I refer to Eve Sedgwick's notion of homosocial as expounded in *Between Men: English Literature and Male Homosocial Desire* (New York: Columbia University Press, 1985).
9. Michiko Kakutani in a review for the *New York Times*, 2 May 1995, focuses on the gimmicky nature of the reverse narrative, which

blunts 'its larger moral ambitions'.

10. James Buchan, 'The Return of Dr Death', *Spectator*, 28 Sept. 1991.
11. Will Self, 'An Interview with Martin Amis', *Mississippi Review*, 3 Oct. 1993, 143–69.
12. Sigmund Freud, *The Interpretation of Dreams*, ed. Ritchie Robertson, trans. Joyce Crick (Oxford: Oxford University Press, [1913] 1999).
13. Steven Spielberg's adaptation of Thomas Keneally's *Schindler's Ark* (retitled as *Schindler's List* for the film) was one recent and very popular dramatization of the Holocaust when Amis published *Time's Arrow*. Spielberg attempted his own kind of defamiliarization by using predominantly black and white cinematography for the film.
14. Self, 'An Interview with Martin Amis'.
15. Roland Barthes, *S/Z*, trans. R. Miller (London: Jonathan Cape, 1975).
16. See Peter Hoffmann, *The History of the German Resistance 1933–1945* (Montreal: McGill-Queen's University Press, 1996); and in fiction, Hans Fallada's *Alone in Berlin*, trans. Michael Hoffman (Harmondsworth: Penguin, 2009), originally published in German as *Jeder Stirbt Für Sich Allein* in 1947.

CHAPTER 5. MID-LIFE CRISES: *THE INFORMATION* AND *NIGHT TRAIN*

1. James Diedrick, 'Amis Agonistes', in *Understanding Martin Amis*, 2nd edn (Columbia: University of South Carolina Press, [1995] 2004), 143–57.
2. This theme of masculine violence being related to frustrated sexuality is also pursued in *Yellow Dog*, and some of his writing on Islamic fundamentalism in the 2000s. See the discussion of this in Chapter 6.
3. William Wordsworth, 'Ode: Intimations of Immortality from Recollections of Early Childhood', in *Wordsworth: Peotical Works*, ed. Thomas Hutchinson (Oxford: Oxford University Press, 1904), 460–2.
4. 'I Look Into My Glass', in *The Complete Poems of Thomas Hardy*, ed. J. Gibson (London: Macmillan, 1976), 81.
5. One of the symptoms of Richard's mid-life crisis is that he is convinced that he smells of shit, and reads innocent comments by his son and others at the Warlock Sports Centre as indications of this (I 226–7, 243).
6. The narrator informs the reader in one section that his initials are M. A., suggesting that Amis is presenting himself as a constructed

narrator, in a way similar to the incorporation of the character 'Martin Amis' in *Money*, and the use of the metafictional references to M. A. in *London Fields* (*I* 63). Later he discusses the nature of being 5′ 5″ and having a taller brother who calls him 'Mart', both of which are true of Amis.

7. In an interview with Will Self in 1995, Amis comments that he is currently working on a novel that eventually becomes *The Information*, that is 'completely realistic', 'An Interview with Martin Amis', *Mississippi Review*, Oct. 1993, 143–69.
8. The narrator somewhat sardonically writes: 'All writers, all book people, were Labour, which was one of the reasons why they got on so well' (I 22); and in Gwyn's case this was 'Obvious not from the ripply cornices twenty feet above their heads, not from the brass lamps or the military plumpness of the leather-topped desk. Obvious because Gwyn was what he was, a writer, in England, at the end of the twentieth century' (I 21).
9. I have previously discussed the concept of meta-criticism in a chapter on Doris Lessing's *The Golden Notebook*, in Alice Ridout and Susan Watkins (eds) *Doris Lessing: Crossing Boundaries* (London: Continuum, 2010), 44–60.
10. The success is implicit in Gal Aplanalp's palindromic name that merges 'A-plan' and alp. It is significant, however, that this character is treated rather sympathetically in the novel, revealing perhaps more of Richard's short-sightedness in not adapting to the new literary culture of which she is representative. Amis famously moved to a new agent, Andrew Wylie, just before the publication of *The Information*, leaving his long-time agent Pat Kavanagh, the then-wife of British novelist Julian Barnes, and sparking a break in the previous friendship of the two writers. It is tempting to read the Richard/Gwyn rivalry as indicative of the rift between Amis and Barnes, although it is clear that neither of them correspond well to the Richard or Gwyn figures in terms of their fiction. Andrew Wylie was able to secure a large advance for *The Information*. Pat Kavanagh died in 2008.
11. Richard Menke, 'Mimesis and Informatics in *The Information*' in Gavin Keulks (ed.), *Martin Amis: Postmodernism and Beyond* (Basingstoke: Palgrave Macmillan, 2006), 137–57.
12. James Diedrick notes how the opening paragraph of *Night Train* bookends Mike's identity as a police woman. Diedrick, *Understanding Martin Amis*, 162.
13. Ibid. 164–5.
14. Michel Maffesoli, *The Time of the Tribes: The Decline of Individualism in Mass Society*, trans. Don Smith (London: Sage, 1996).
15. Although Jennifer commits suicide, the novel makes it clear that

this a crime story as Jennifer's actions are deemed criminal in Chicago: 'In our city [. . .] what she did was a crime' (*NT* 60).

16. The fact that Jennifer set up this meeting in the 'Decoy Room' of a hotel called The Mallard alerts Mike to Jennifer's darkly playful manipulation of the inevitable investigation of her suicide.
17. As he writes in *Experience* this focus on self-destruction was precipitated by his learning the fact that he had a daughter, Delilah Seale, he did not know about from a relationship with Leonora Seale, who committed suicide in 1978. It has subsequently transpired that Amis did meet with Leonora in 1977 and was informed that he was the father of Delilah, but promised on her request to keep this knowledge to himself.
18. That this is an important aspect of the suicide can be identified in an interview with Will Self from 1993, in which Amis, in discussing *Time's Arrow*, makes the link between suicide and the contemplation of death and relates it to the La Rochefoucault quotation, Self, 'An Interview with Martin Amis', 143–69.

CHAPTER 6. THE WILD DOGS: *YELLOW DOG* AND *HOUSE OF MEETINGS*

1. Although, as argued in the last chapter, this move to a realist framework can be seen in Amis's novels of the 1990s.
2. 'State of England' was first published in *New Yorker* in 1996.
3. Amis comments: 'I came back to it on September 10, 2001, and was settling down and finding it was marvellous freedom to be writing fiction again, and not to be limited by the truth or actuality as you are with a memoir. Then the event happened and, like every other writer on earth, the next day I was considering a change in occupation', Gerald Isaaman, 'It's a Mad, Mad World that Inspires Martin', in *Camden New Journal*, 30 Sept. 2003.
4. Dominic Head, *State of the Nation*; Gavin Keulks, 'W(h)ither Postmodernism: Late Amis', in Gavin Keulks (ed.), *Martin Amis: Postmodernism and Beyond* (Basingstoke: Palgrave Macmillan, 2006), 158–79; Philip Tew, *The Contemporary British Novel*, 2nd edn (London: Continuum, 2007), 202–3.
5. James Diedrick, *Understanding Martin Amis*, 2nd edn (Columbia: University of South Carolina Press, [1995] 2004), 228.
6. Martin Amis, *The Second Plane: September 11: 2001–2007* (London: Jonathan Cape, 2008), 101. Note that the subtitle of Amis's book implicitly suggests that the 9/11 attacks continue to influence across the decade.

7. Martin Amis, 'The Islamist', in *The Second Plane*, 189–94, 192.
8. Camden is a district in the north-west of central London that is famed for its youth culture and alternative night life.
9. Part of the backstory we are given is the fact that Mick Meo, the person who Xan thought was his real father, has been murdered on Andrews's instigation.
10. Despite claiming that he is a feminist, it is clear in this novel that Amis is reproducing traditional ideas of gendered spaces. Amis's gender politics are discussed in further detail in Chapter 7 with respect to *The Pregnant Widow*.
11. Keulks, 'W(h)ither Postmodernism: Late Amis'.
12. Amis is equally keen to criticize the logic behind Bush's 'theological' reasoning (or rather the irrational) for the invasion of Iraq as a form of masculine revenge. See 'The Wrong War' in *The Second Plane*, 21–9.
13. *The Morning Lark* is modelled on a number of British newspapers (only slightly exaggerated) such as the *The Daily Star*, *The Sport* and to a lesser extent *The Sun*, *The Daily Mirror* and the now defunct *News of the World*. Indeed the phone hacking scandal of 2011 that caused the closure of the *News of the World* in many ways vindicates Amis's critique of the 'Yellow' press in Britain during this period.
14. The plot devices can be a little clunky in the novel. It turns out that He Zizhen, the King's illicit lover, has been hired by Joseph Andrews as an elaborate form of blackmail, so that Andrews can return to Britain to die without being arrested. He Zizhen is also the shadowy figure that appears in the footage of Princess Victoria bathing naked in the Yellow House. It would appear that Amis is here following the Dickensian convention of suggesting a society that is linked from top to bottom, and that the corruption, pornography and violence contaminates all levels. Dickens adopts a similar scenario in *Bleak House*, in which the Baronet and Lady Dedlock are connected by way of Esther Summerson, the novel's heroine, to Tom the road sweeper. The conduit for the connection is in Dickens's case a similarly corrupting metaphor to Amis's use of porn in *Yellow Dog* – that of cholera.
15. Diedrick, Understanding *Martin Amis*, 240.
16. As M. John Harrison has written in a review of the novel: 'the central irony of most Amis novels [...] is [that] the issue of storytelling is always the issue of character'; 'Decline and Fall: House of Meetings by Martin Amis', *Guardian*, 30 Sept. 2006, 7.
17. The narrator also cites several giants of Russian literature who seem to support his generalizing outlook of the Russian psyche: 'Gogol, Dostoevsky, Tolstoy: each of them insisted on a Russian God, a specifically Russian God' (*HM* 116).

18. Roland Barthes, *S/Z*, trans. R. Miller (London: Jonathan Cape, 1975). Barthes is mainly concerned with the way in which the narrative scene and characters are left up to the reader to decide, whereas Amis extends this situation into the arena of the moral, the ethical and the political.
19. Amis is borrowing here from that other great novel of the victory of totalitarian power over the human: George Orwell's *Nineteen Eighty-Four*. The 'house of meetings' serves as a similar structural device as Room 101 in Orwell's novel – the place where the final and terrible power of the state over the individual is acknowledged by the one individual who has until that point managed to stand up to it. Orwell's novel appears as an intertextual reference in a number of Amis's novels including *Other People*, *Money* and *London Fields*.
20. Theodor Adorno, 'Cultural Criticism and Society', in *Prisms*, trans. Samuel and Shierry Weber (Cambridge, Mass.: MIT Press, 1967), 34.

CHAPTER 7. CAST OF CROOKS: *THE PREGNANT WIDOW* AND *LIONEL ASBO*

1. The title of this chapter is taken from Philip Larkin's poem 'Going, going' which includes a conservative sentiment that chimes well with some of the ideas in Amis's later fiction, Philip Larkin, *Selected Poems* (London: Marvell Press and Faber and Faber, 1988), 189–90.
2. Stephen Moss, 'Martin Amis: "I don't want to tread carefully"', *Guardian*, 1 Feb. 2010. Amis talks about the 'silver tsunami' of ageing people in Britain, potentially generating an age war in future decades.
3. Kate Mitchell made this point in unpublished comments made in response to a paper on Martin Amis delivered at the conference What Happens Now: 21st Century Writing in English, University of Lincoln, 16–18 July 2012. The paper Mitchell was responding to was Ayse Naz Bulamur, 'Scheherazade in Western Palace: Martin Amis, *The Pregnant Widow*', delivered 16 July 2012.
4. In an interview with Stephen Moss from 2010, Amis claims 'I've been a passionate feminist since the mid-eighties', Moss, 'Martin Amis: "I don't want to tread carefully"'.
5. Given the novel's focus on the sexual revolution, it is significant that there is little representation of gay and/or lesbian identity. Keith's friend in Italy, Whittaker, is gay, but he is only a minor character and the focus is clearly on Keith's 'het' relationships with women (PW 11).

6. Adam Mars-Jones has offered a perceptive criticism of Amis's title suggesting that what it produces is a 'poorly handled' image of Alexander Herzen's original, 'Anti-Dad', *London Review of Books*, 21 June 2012.
7. This study steers away from analysing the novels in relation to Amis's life story, but he has discussed the character of Violet with respect to his younger sister Sally, who died in 1970. If you are interested in the kind of literary analysis that tries to map the author's real-life relationships with the fiction, then Richard Bradford's somewhat salacious biography is useful.
8. Brian Finney has argued that the novel is primarily concerned with the impossibility of writing about real, historical life, substituting this with a kind of literary genre of 'Life' which needs plot and characters for us to make sense of it. See Brian Finney, 'Life and Other Genres: Martin Amis's *The Pregnant Widow*, *The Martin Amis Web*, http://www.martinamisweb.com/scholarship_files/finney_pregwid.pdf, accessed 17 Aug. 2012.
9. Amis pursued a similar literary history of sexual mores in the short story 'Let Me Count the Times' in which the narrator imagines having sex with a series of female characters in classic literary texts, 'Let Me Count the Times' in *Heavy Water and Other Stories* (London: Jonathan Cape, 1998), 75–93.
10. Another connection the novel has with *Yellow Dog* is the threatening canine imagery. One of the motifs is the phrase 'who let the dogs in?' As in the previous novel, dogs refer to the potential violence and brute animalistic nature that is conveyed in aspects of contemporary masculinity in Britain. Lionel owns three pairs of dogs in the course of the novel, each pair being trained to be increasingly violent:

    The dogs: their sloppy faces, their tongues hanging from the corners of their jaws like something half-eaten, their blind eyes and staring nostrils, their forelimbs planted stupidly far apart. They thickly barked. And they weren't barking out – they were barking in.
    Fuckoff, said Joe.
    Fuckoff, said Jeff (LA 55)

    The pit-bulls are anthropomorphized in their barking, but the novel also operates the other way: Lionel's brute aggression dovetailing with that of his dogs. The novel, however, makes it clear that this aggressive characteristic is cultural and not natural. Lionel spends a great deal of thought about training his dogs to be violent, feeding them on Tabasco sauce and bottles of lager to give them aggression-inducing hangovers. It is not hard to see that such a diet is also the stock intake of stereotypical images of contemporary urban (white) men. When the last pair of dogs in the novel, Jak and Jek, are being looked after by Des and Dawn their softer side is cultivated. The final dénouement revolves around the threat these two dogs offer to the baby Cilla once they have been taken away by Lionel and re-hardened in his usual manner.

11. *Crimewatch* is a popular UK BBC TV show that asks viewers to contact the police in relation to crimes they may have information about.
12. Owen Jones, in particular, offered a mini-critique of *Lionel Asbo* by way of an introduction to an interview with Amis on the BBC's *Culture Show*. Jones criticized the novel in the following terms: 'Martin Amis is writing about a cardboard cut-out of broken Britain, and he's caricaturing people he's in no position of knowing anything about'. Unfortunately, Jones goes on to criticize (caricature) George Bernard Shaw, Virginia Woolf and H. G. Wells for comments about the working class, who he takes out of context, which somewhat undermines his own admonition of Amis, *The Culture Show*, BBC 2, first broadcast 20 June 2012.
13. Owen Jones, *Chavs: the Demonization of the Working Class* (London: Verso, 2011), 5–6.
14. Amanda Craig identifies Lionel as a 'cartoon of a chav' in a review for the *Independent*, 10 June 2012. It will be interesting to note whether future editions retain the cartoonish nature of the front cover, or elect for a more realist image as the historical context moves further into the past.
15. This manipulation of the reader's sympathies towards what appears at first to be a wholly reprehensible character is also a feature of *Money*, and its portrayal of John Self.
16. The model here is Dickens, not George Eliot, in that the form of realism used is one in which a recognizable social and geographical space is overlaid with characters that extend beyond the conventional towards the exaggerated and grotesque. That Dickens is identified as an influence in the style of *Lionel Asbo* can be seen in the naming of institutions and streets in the novel, for example Squeers Free School, Murdstone Road, Jupes Lane, Carker Square, are all intertextual references to characters in Dickens's fiction.
17. *The Culture Show*, 20 June 2012. Amis is referring here to the Horatian model for imaginative art: 'aut prodess uolent aut delectare poetae/aut simul et iucunda et idonea dicere uitae', which can be translated as 'The aim of a poet is either to benefit or delight, or to speak words that are simultaneously pleasing and instructive', Horace, 'Epistle to the Pisones (*Ars Poetica*)', in *Epistles Book II*, ed. Niall Rudd (Cambridge: Cambridge University Press, 1989), 69, ll.333–4.

Select Bibliography

WORKS BY MARTIN AMIS

Novels

The Rachel Papers (London: Jonathan Cape, 1973)
Dead Babies (London: Jonathan Cape, 1975)
Success (London: Jonathan Cape, 1978)
Other People: A Mystery (London: Jonathan Cape, 1981)
Money: A Suicide Note (London: Jonathan Cape, 1984)
London Fields (London: Jonathan Cape, 1989)
Time's Arrow, or The Nature of the Offence (London: Jonathan Cape, 1991)
The Information (London: Flamingo, 1995)
Night Train (London: Jonathan Cape, 1997)
Yellow Dog (London: Jonathan Cape, 2003)
House of Meetings (London: Jonathan Cape, 2006)
The Pregnant Widow (London: Jonathan Cape, 2010)
Lionel Asbo: State of England (London: Jonathan Cape, 2012)

Short Story Collections

Einstein's Monsters (London: Jonathan Cape, 1987)
Heavy Water and Other Stories (London: Jonathan Cape, 1998)

Autobiography

Experience (London: Jonathan Cape, 2000)
Koba the Dread: Laughter and the Twenty Million (London: Jonathan Cape, 2002)

Essays, Reviews and Criticism

Invasion of the Space Invaders (London: Hutchinson, 1982)

The Moronic Inferno and Other Visits to America (London: Jonathan Cape, 1986)

Visiting Mrs Nabokov and Other Excursions (London: Jonathan Cape, 1993)

The War Against Cliché: Essays and Reviews 1971–2000 (London: Jonathan Cape, 2001)

'Against Dryness', in *On Modern British Fiction* (Oxford: Oxford University Press, 2002), 265–9

The Second Plane: September 11, 2001–2007 (London: Jonathan Cape, 2008)

'Force of Love: Pride and Prejudice by Jane Austen', in Susannah Carson (ed.), *A Truth Universally Acknowledged: 33 Great Writers on Why We Read Jane Austen* (New York: Random House, 2009), 83–9

'Divine Levity', *Times Literary Supplement*, 23 & 30 Dec. 2011, 3–5

CRITICAL STUDIES

Alexander, Victoria N., 'Martin Amis: Between the Influences of Bellow and Nabokov', *Antioch Review*, 52/4 (1994), 580–90.

Almazán, Eva, 'A Casa dos Encontros Dixitais: A Tecnoloxía ao Rescate da Tradutora Editorial en Apuros', *Viceversa: Revista Galega de Traducción*, 13 (2007), 305–16.

Altnöder, Sonja, 'Die Stadt als Körper: Materialität und Diskursivität in zwei London-Romanen', in Wolfgang Hallet and Birgit Neumann (eds), *Raum und Bewegung in der Literatur: Die Literaturwissenschaften und der Spatial Turn* (Bielefeld: Transcript, 2009), 299–318.

Anelli, Sara, 'Counterfactual Holocausts: Robert Harris' *Fatherland* and Martin Amis' *Time's Arrow*', *Textus: English Studies in Italy*, 20/2 (2007), 407–32.

Ashley, Leonard R. N., '"Names Are Awfully Important": The Onomastics of Satirical Comment in Martin Amis's *Money: A Suicide Note*', *Literary Onomastics Studies* 14 (1987), 1–48.

Baker, Robert S., 'Kingsley Amis and Martin Amis: the Ironic Inferno of British Satire', *Contemporary Literature*, 46/3 (2005), 544–54.

Bawar, Bruce, 'Martin Amis on America', *New Criterion*, 5/2, 20–6.

Begley, Jon, 'Satirizing the Carnival of Postmodern Capitalism: The Transatlantic and Dialogic Structure of Martin Amis's *Money*', *Contemporary Literature* 45/1 (2004), 79–105.

Bentley, Nick, *Radical Fictions: The English Novel in the 1950s* (Oxford: Peter Lang, 2007).

———, 'Narrative Forms: Postmodernism and Realism', in *Contemporary British Fiction* (Edinburgh: Edinburgh University Press, 2008), 30–64.

———, 'Satiromania: Postmodern Satire in Martin Amis's *Dead Babies*', *Critical Engagements: A Journal of Criticism and Theory*, 3/2 (2009), 53–72.

Bényei, Tamas, 'Allegory and Allegoresis in *Money*', *The Proceedings of the First Conference of the Hungarian Society for the Study of English*, Vol. 1 (Debrecen: Institute of English and American Studies, 1995), 182–7.

———, 'The Passion of John Self: Allegory, Economy, and Expenditure in Martin Amis's *Money*', in Gavin Keulks (ed.), *Martin Amis: Postmodernism and Beyond* (Basingstoke: Palgrave Macmillan, 2006), 36–54.

Bernard, Catherine, 'Dismembering/Remembering Mimesis: Martin Amis, Graham Swift', in Theo D'Haen and Hans Bertens (eds), *British Postmodern Fiction* (Amsterdam and Atlanta, GA: Rodopi, 1993), 121–44.

———, 'Under the Dark Sun of Melancholia: Writing and Loss in *The Information*', in Keulks (ed.), *Martin Amis: Postmodernism and Beyond*, 117–36.

Beville, Maria, 'Passages in Time Traversed, Passages in Text Unwritten: A Theoretical Approach to Martin Amis's *Time's Arrow*', in Maeve Tynan, Maria Belville and Marita Ryan (eds), *Passages: Movements and Moments in Text and Theory* (Newcastle upon Tyne: Cambridge Scholars, 2009), 19–30.

Bigsby, Christopher, 'Martin Amis', in Malcom Bradbury and Judy Cook (eds), *New Writing* (London: Minerva, 1992), 169–84.

Botting, Fred, 'From Excess to the New World Order', in Nick Bentley (ed.), *British Fiction of the 1990s* (London and New York: Routledge, 2005), 21–41.

Bradley, Arthur and Andrew Tate, 'Martin Amis and the War for Cliché', in *The New Atheist Novel: Fiction, Philosophy and Polemic after 9/11* (London Continuum, 210), 36–55.

———, 'The New Atheist Novel: Literature, Religion, and Terror in Amis and McEwan', *Yearbook of English Studies*, 39/1–2 (2009), 20–38.

Brook, Susan, 'The Female Form, Sublimation, and Nicola Six', in Keulks (ed.), *Martin Amis: Postmodernism and Beyond*, 87–100.

Brooker, Joseph, 'The Middle Years of Martin Amis', in Rod Mengham and Philip Tew (eds.) *British Fiction Today* (London and New York: Continuum, 2006), 3–14.

———, 'License is Given: *Money* and the Menace of Comedy', Critical Engagements: A *Journal of Criticism and Theory*, 3/2 (2009), 73–90.

———, 'Sado-Monetarism: Thatcherite Subjects in Alasdair Gray and Martin Amis', *Textual Practice*, 26/1 (2012), 135–54.

Brooks, Neil, '"My Heart Really Goes Out to Me": The Self-Indulgent Highway to Adulthood in *The Rachel Papers*', in Keulks (ed.), *Martin Amis: Postmodernism and Beyond*, 9–21.

Brown, Richard, 'Postmodern Americas in the Fiction of Angela Carter, Martin Amis and Ian McEwan', in Anna Massa and Alistair Stead (eds), *Forked Tongues? Comparing Twentieth Century British and American Literature* (London and New York: Longman, 1994), 92–110.

Chatman, Seymour, 'Backwards', in *Narrative*, 17/1 (2009) 31–55.

Childs, Peter, 'Martin Amis: Lucre, Love, and Literature', in *Contemporary Novelists: British Fiction Since 1970* (Basingstoke and New York: Palgrave, 2005), 35–57.

Cowley, Jason, 'Martin Amis, *The Information*', in Liam McIlvanney, Ray Ryan (eds), *The Good of the Novel* (London and New York: Continuum, 2011), 91–109.

Crews, Brian, 'Martin Amis and the Postmodern Grotesque', *Modern Language Review*, 105/3 (2010), 641–59.

Däwes, Birgit, '"Close neighbours to the unimaginable": Literary Projections of Terrorists' Perspectives (Martin Amis, John Updike, Don DeLillo)', *Amerikastudien/American Studies*, 55/3 (2010), 495–517.

Dern, John A., *Martians, Monsters and Madonnas: Fiction and Form in the World of Martin Amis* (New York: Peter Lang, 2000).

Diedrick, James, *Understanding Martin Amis*, 2nd edn (Columbia: University of South Carolina Press, [1995] 2004).

———, 'The Fiction of Martin Amis: Patriarchy and its Discontents', in Richard J. Hand, Rod Mengham and Philip Tew (eds), *Contemporary British Fiction* (Cambridge: Polity, 2003), 239–55.

———, 'J .G. Ballard's "Inner Space" and the Early Fiction of Martin Amis', in Keulks (ed.), *Martin Amis: Postmodernism and Beyond*, 180–96.

———, and M. Hunter Hayes, 'Nonfiction by Martin Amis, 1971-2005', in Keulks (ed.), *Martin Amis: Postmodernism and Beyond*, 211–34.

Doan, Laura L., '"Sexy Greedy Is the Late Eighties": Power Systems in Amis's *Money* and Churchill's *Serious Money*', *Minnesota Review*, 34/5 (1990), 69–80.

Duffy, Brian, 'From a Good Firm Knot to a Mess of Loose Ends: Identity and Solution in Martin Amis' *Night Train*', in Marieke Krajenbrink and Kate M. Quinn (eds), *Investigating Identities: Questions of Identity in Contemporary International Crime Fiction* (Amsterdam: Rodopi, 2009), 311–24.

Duggan, Robert, 'Big-Time Shakespeare and the Joker in the Pack: The Intrusive Author in Martin Amis's *Money*' in *Journal of Narrative Theory*, 39/1 (2009), 86–110.

Edmondson, Elie A., 'Martin Amis Writes Postmodern Man', *Critique: Studies in Contemporary Fiction*, 42/2 (2001), 145–54.

Elias, Amy J., 'Meta-*mimesis*? The Problem of British Postmodern Fiction', in Theo D'Haen and Hans Bertens (eds), *British Post-*

modernist Fiction, (Amsterdam and Atlanta, GA: Rodopi, 1993), 931.

Finney, Brian, 'Narrative and Narrated Homicides in Martin Amis's *Other People* and *London Fields*', *Critique: Studies in Contemporary Fiction*, 37/1 (1995), 3–15.

———, Martin Amis's *Time's Arrow* and the Postmodern Sublime', in Keulks (ed.), *Martin Amis: Postmodernism and Beyond*, 101–16.

———, 'Violence in the Work of Martin Amis', in Will Wright and Steven Kaplan (eds), *The Image of Violence in Literature, Media, and Society II* (Pueblo, Col.: Colorado State University-Pueblo, 2007), 193–7.

———, *Martin Amis* (London and New York: Routledge, 2008).

———, 'Life and Other Genres: Martin Amis's *The Pregnant Widow*', Internet article, http://www.martinamisweb.com/scholarship_files/finney_pregwid.pdf, accessed 18 Dec. 2012, California State University, Long Beach (2012).

———, 'What's Amis in Contemporary British Fiction? Martin Amis's *Money* and *Time's Arrow*', http://www.martinamisweb.com/scholarship_files/finney_whatsamis.pdf, accessed 18 Dec. 2012, California State University, Long Beach (1999).

Fordham, Finn, 'Nabokov on the Road to *Money*', *Textual Practice*, 26/1 (2012), 43–62.

Fortin-Tournès, Anne-Laure, 'The War against Cliché de Martin Amis: l'essai critique comme embrassement amoureux de la littérature', *Études Britanniques Contemporaines*, 38 (2010), 45–56.

Galef, David, 'The Importance of Being Amis, Revisited', *Southwest Review*, 87/4 (2002), 554–64.

Ganteau, Jean-Michel, 'Violence Biting Its Own Tail: Martin Amis's *Yellow Dog*', in Alain-Phillip Durand and Naomi Mandel (eds), *Novels of the Contemporary Extreme* (London and New York: Continuum, 2006), 132–42.

———, '"If you like, we play detective": intrigues en souffrance chez Peter Ackroyd, Martin Amis et Kazuo Ishiguro', *Études Anglaises*, 64/4 (2011), 415–26.

Germanà, Monica, 'Beyond the Gaps: Postmodernist Representations of the Metropolis', in Christine Berberich, Neil Campbell and Robert Hudson (eds), *Land and Identity: Theory, Memory, and Practice* (Amsterdam: Rodopi, 2012), 213–34.

Glaz, Adam, 'The Self in Time: Reversing the Irreversible in Martin Amis's *Time's Arrow*', *Journal of Literary Semantics*, 35/2 (2006), 105–22.

Gluhbegovich, Zia, 'The Tarnished Mirror of the World: London in the Intertextual Web of Martin Amis's *London Fields*', *Literary London Journal*, 2/2 (2004).

Greaney, Michael, 'The Novelist on Holiday: Martin Amis and the Short Story', in Alisa Cox (ed.), *The Short Story* (Newcastle upon Tyne:

Cambridge Scholars, 2008), 130–41.

Harris, Greg, 'Men Giving Birth to New World Orders: Martin Amis's *Time's Arrow*', *Studies in the Novel*, 31/4 (1999), 489–505.

Hawkes, David, 'Martin Amis', in G. Stade and C. Howard (eds), *British Writers, Supplement IV* (New York: Scribner's, 1997), 25–44.

Hayes, Hunter M., 'A Reluctant Leavisite: Martin Amis's "Higher Journalism"', in Keulks (ed.), *Martin Amis: Postmodernism and Beyond*, 197–210.

Holmes, Frederick, 'The Death of the Author as Cultural Critique in *London Fields*', in Ricardo Miguel Alonso (ed.), *Powerless Fictions? Ethics, Cultural Critique, and American Fiction in the Age of Postmodernism* (Amsterdam and Atlanta, GA: Rodopi, 1996), 53–62.

Hutchinson, Colin, 'Transatlantic Class: Martin Amis and the "Special Relationship" of the 1980s', *Symbiosis: A Journal of Anglo-American Literary Relations*, 12/1 (2008), 59–75.

James, David, '"Style is Morality?" Aesthetics and Politics in the Amis Era', *Textual Practice*, 26/1 (2012), 11–25.

Joffe, Phil, 'Language Damage: Nazis and Naming in Martin Amis's *Time's Arrow*', *Nomina Africana: Journal of the Names Society of South Africa*, 9/2 (1995), 1–10.

Juhász, Tamás, 'Murderous Parents, Trustful Children: The Parental Trap in Imre Kertész's *Fatelessness* and Martin Amis's *Time's Arrow*', *Comparative Literature Studies*, 46/4 (2009), 645–66.

Kempner, Brandon, '"Blow the World Back Together": Literary Nostalgia, 9/11, and Terrorism in Seamus Heaney, Chris Cleave, and Martin Amis', in Cara Cilano (ed.), *From Solidarity to Schisms: 9/11 and after in Fiction and Film from Outside the US* (Amsterdam: Rodopi, 2009), 53–74.

Keulks, Gavin, *Father and Son: Kingsley Amis, Martin Amis, and the British Novel Since 1950* (Madison, Wisc.: University of Wisconsin Press, 2003).

———, (ed.), *Martin Amis: Postmodernism and Beyond* (Basingstoke: Palgrave Macmillan, 2006).

———, 'W(h)ither Postmodernism: Late Amis', in Keulks (ed.), *Martin Amis: Postmodernism and Beyond*, 158–79.

LaRose, Nicole, 'Reading *The Information* on Martin Amis's London', *Critique: Studies in Contemporary Fiction*, 46/2 (2005), 160–76.

Larsonneur, Claire, 'Revisiting London's Monuments: Sidelining Graham Swift, Ian McEwan, Martin Amis', in Vanessa Guignery and François Gallix (eds), *(Re-) Mapping London: Visions of the Metropolis in the Contemporary Novel in English* (Paris: Publibook, 2008), 113–27.

McCarthy, Dermot, 'The Limits of Irony: The Chronillogical World of Martin Amis's *Time's Arrow*', *War, Literature and the Arts*, 11/1 (1999), 294–320.

Mackintosh, Alasdair, 'Martin Amis and the Language of Science Fiction', *New York Review of Science Fiction*, 23/7 (2011), 10–17.

Mączyńska, Magdalena, 'Writing the Writer: The Question of Authorship in the Novels of Martin Amis', in Michael J. Meyer (ed.), *Literature and the Writer* (Amsterdam and Atlanta, GA: Rodopi, 2004), 191–207.

———, This Monstrous City: Urban Visionary Satire in the Fiction of Martin Amis, Will Self, China Miéville, and Maggie Gee', *Contemporary Literature*, 51/1 (2010), 58–86.

Mars-Jones, Adam, *Venus Envy* (London: Chatto and Windus, 1990).

Marsh, Nicky: 'Taking the Maggie: Money, Sovereignty, and Masculinity in British Fiction of the Eighties', *Modern Fiction Studies*, 53/4 (2007), 845–66.

———, '*Money*'s Doubles: Reading, Fiction and Finance Capital', *Textual Practice*, 26/1 (2012), 115–33.

Martínez-Alfaro, María Jesús, 'Experimental Fiction and the Ethics of a Verité: The Encounter with the Other in Martin Amis' *Night Train*', in Susana Onega and Jean-Michel Ganteau (eds), *The Ethical Component in Experimental British Fiction since the 1960s*, (Newcastle upon Tyne: Cambridge Scholars, 2007), 131–49.

———, 'A Look into the Abyss: The Unsolvable Enigma of the Self and the Challenges of Metaphysical Detection in Martin Amis's *Night Train*', *Journal of Narrative Theory*, 40/1 (2010), 108–28.

———, 'Where Madness Lies: Holocaust Representation and the Ethics of Form in Martin Amis's *Time's Arrow*', *DQR Studies in Literature*, 48 (2011), 127–54.

Menke, Richard, 'Narrative Reversals and the Thermodynamics of History in Martin Amis's *Time's Arrow*', *Modern Fiction Studies*, 44/4 (1998) 959–80.

———, 'Mimesis and Informatics in *The Information*, in Keulks (ed.), *Martin Amis: Postmodernism and Beyond*, 137–57.

Mills, Sara, 'Working With Sexism: What Can Feminist Text Analysis Do?', in Peter Verdonk and Jean Jacques Weer (eds), *Twentieth Century Fiction: From Text to Context* (London and New York: Routledge, 1995), 206–19.

Miracky, James, 'Hope Lost or Hyped Lust? Gendered Representations in 1980s Britain in Margaret Drabble's *The Radiant Way* and Martin Amis's *Money*', *Critique*, 44/2 (2003), 136–43.

Moran, Joe, 'Artists and Verbal Mechanics: Martin Amis's *The Information*', *Critique: Studies in Contemporary Fiction*, 41/4 (2000), 307–17.

Merritt, Moseley, 'Amis, Father and Son', in Brian W. Shaffer (ed.) *A Companion to the British and Irish Novel 1945–2000* (Oxford: Blackwell, 2005), 302–13.

Mitchell, Kaye, 'Self-Abuse: The Pornography of Postmodern Life in

Money', *Textual Practice*, 26/1 (2012), 79–97.

Moyle, David, 'Beyond the Black Hole: The Emergence of Science Fiction Themes in the Recent Work of Martin Amis', *Extrapolation*, 36/4 (1995), 305–15.

Nakanishi, Wendy Jones, 'Nihilism or Nonsense? The Postmodern Fiction of Martin Amis and Haruki Murakami', *Electronic Journal of Contemporary Japanese Studies*, 6/1 (2006).

Nash, John, 'Fiction May Be a Legal Paternity: Martin Amis's *The Information*', *English*, 45/183 (1996), 213–24.

Norman, Will, 'Killing the Crime Novel: Martin Amis's *Night Train*, Genre and Literary Fiction', *Journal of Modern Literature*, 35/1 (2011), 37–59.

Oertel, Daniel, 'Effects of Garden-Pathing in Marin Amis's Novels *Time's Arrow* and *Night Train*', *Miscelanea: A Journal of English and American Studies*, 22 (2001), 123–40.

Padhi, Shanti, 'Bed and Bedlam: The Hard-Core Extravaganzas of Martin Amis', *The Literary Half-Yearly*, 23/1 (1982), 36–42.

Parker, Emma, 'Money Makes the Man: Gender and Sexuality in Martin Amis's *Money*', in Keulks (ed.), *Martin Amis: Postmodernism and Beyond*, 55–70.

Phelan, James, 'The Ethics and Aesthetics of Backward Narration in Martin Amis's *Time's Arrow*', in Jakob Lothe, Susan Rubin Suleiman and James Phelan (eds), *After Testimony: The Ethics and Aesthetics of Holocaust Narrative for the Future* (Columbus, Oh.: Ohio State University Press, 2012), 120–39.

Piatek, Beata, '"Bullshit TV Conversations" or Intertextuality in *Night Train*', in Zygmunt Mazur and Richard Utz (eds), *Homo Narrans: Texts and Essays in Honor of Jerome Klinkowitz* (Krakow: Jagielonian University Press, 2004), 157–73.

Powell, Neil, 'What Life Is: The Novels of Martin Amis', *PN Review*, 20, 7/6 (1981), 42–5.

Reynolds, Margaret and Jonathan Noakes, *Martin Amis: The Rachel Papers, London Fields, Time's Arrow, Experience* (London: Vintage, 2003).

Riviere, Francesca, 'Martin Amis', *Paris Review*, 40/146 (1998), 108–35.

Setz, Cathryn, '*Money* Men', *Textual Practice*, 26/1 (2012), 63–77.

Silva-Campañón, Carlos, 'Through the Looking Glass: America in Martin Amis's *Money: A Suicide Note*' *Atlantis*, 26/2 (2004), 87–96.

Simõe, Elsa, 'Lessons in humiliation in three mystery novels: Martin Amis' *Money*, *The Information* and *Night Train*', Proceedings of the APEAA Conference, 2008, http://www.martinamisweb.com/scholarship_files/simoes_lessons.pdf, accessed 18 Dec. 2012.

Smith, Penny, 'Hell Innit: The Millennium in Alasdair Grey's *Lanark*, Martin Amis's *London Fields*, and Shena Mackay's *Dunedin*', *Essays and Studies*, 48 (1995), 115–28.

Stokes, Peter, 'Martin Amis and the Postmodern Suicide: Tracing the Postnuclear Narrative at the Fin de Millénium', *Critique: Studies in Contemporary Fiction*, 38/4 (1997), 300–11.

Szczekalla, Michael, '"Under Western Eyes": Eastern Europe and the Soviet Union in the Fiction of Martin Amis, Nicholas Shakespeare and Carl Tighe', in Barbara Korte, Eva Ulrike Pirker and Sissy Helff (eds), *Facing the East in the West: Images of Eastern Europe in British Literature, Film and Culture* (Amsterdam: Rodopi, 2010), 397–410.

Tew, Philip, 'Martin Amis and Late-twentieth-century Working-class Masculinity: *Money* and *London Fields*', in Keulks (ed.), *Martin Amis: Postmodernism and Beyond*, 71–86.

———, 'Alexithymia and a Broken Plastic Umbrella: Contemporary Culture and Martin Amis's *Money*', *Textual Practice*, 26/1 (2012), 99–114.

Thomas, Susie, 'Posing as a Postmodernist: Race and Class in Martin Amis's *London Fields*', *Literary London Journal* 1/2 (Sept. 2003).

———, and Jesse Thomas, 'Attaboy!: Martin Amis's "The Last Days of Muhammad Atta" and "The Age of Horrorism"', in *Rising East*, 4 May 2006.

Todd, Richard, 'The Intrusive Author in British Postmodern Fiction: The Cases of Alasdair Grey and Martin Amis', in Matei Calinescu and Douwe Fokkema (eds), *Exploring Postmodernism* (Amsterdam and Philadelphia, PA: John Benjamins, 1990), 123–37.

———, 'Looking-Glass Worlds in Martin Amis's Early Fiction: Reflections, Mirror Narcissism, and Doubles', in Keulks (ed.), *Martin Amis: Postmodernism and Beyond*, 22–35.

Tredell Nicolas, *The Fiction of Martin Amis: A Reader's Guide to Essential Criticism* (Basingstoke: Palgrave Macmillan, 2000).

Verrier, Luc, 'Inevitable Yet Impossible Impersonality: Martin Amis's *The Information*' in Christine Reynier and Jean-Michel Ganteau (eds), *Impersonality and Emotion in Twentieth-Century British Literature* (Montpellier: Université Montpellier III, 2005), 273–85.

———, 'L'Etrangeté gothique de l'inanimé dans la fiction de Martin Amis', *Etudes Britanniques Contemporaines: Revue de la Société d'Etudes Anglaises Contemporaines*, 32 (2007) 125–38.

Zahar, Isabelle, 'The Artist as Critic, Style as Ethics: Amis's American Stylists and Self's Stylisation', *Textual Practice*, 26/1 (2012), 27–42.

Zhang, Helong, 'Carnival Desire and Postmodern Cities in Martin Amis's *Money: A Suicide Note*', *Foreign Literature Studies*, 139 (2009), 99–108. (In Chinese)

BIOGRAPHIES

Bradford, Richard, *Martin Amis: The Biography* (London: Constable, 2011).

Howard, Elizabeth Jane, *Slipstream: A Memoir* (London: Pan, 2003).

Leader, Zachary, *The Life of Kingsley Amis* (London: Jonathan Cape, 2006).

Powell, Neil, *Amis & Son: Two Literary Generations* (London: Macmillan, 2008).

REVIEWS AND INTERVIEWS

Adams, Tim, 'Glad to have you back, Keith', *Observer*, 31 Jan. 2010.

Adiga, Aravind, Review of *The Pregnant Widow*, *Sunday Times*, 6 Feb. 2010.

Amidon, Stephen, 'Manipulation of Love and Death', *Financial Times*, 23 Sept. 1989.

Annand, David, 'Review of *Lionel Asbo*', *Telegraph*, 14 June 2012.

Baker, Simon, 'Back to Top Form', *Spectator*, 30 Sept. 2006.

Banville, John, 'Executioner Songs', *New York Review of Books*, 1 March 2007.

Barker, Nicola, 'Review of *Lionel Asbo: State of England*', *Observer*, 13 June 2012.

Barnes, Jonathan, 'Martin Amis's Asbo', *Times Literary Supplement*, 20 June 2012.

Battersby, Eileen, 'Eloquently Outraged Sorrow', *Irish Times*, 14 Oct. 2006.

Birnbaum, Robert, 'Martin Amis: Author of *Yellow Dog* Talks with Robert Birnbaum' *identitytheory.com*, www.identitytheory.com/martin-amis/, (2003), accessed 1 Sept. 2012.

Blades, John, 'A Literary Counterattack on Einstein's "Monsters"', *Chicago Tribune*, 11 June 1987.

Blimes, Alex, '30 Things I've Learned About Terror', *Independent on Sunday*, 8 Oct. 2006.

Bradford, Richard, 'It Happened One Summer', *Spectator*, 6 Feb. 2010.

Bragg, Melvyn, 'Martin Amis', television broadcast, *South Bank Show*, London Weekend Television, 17 Sept. 1989.

———, 'A Novel Experience', *Sunday Times*, 17 Dec. 1989.

Buchan, James, 'The Return of Dr Death', *Spectator*, 28 Sept. 1991.

Byrne, Ciar, 'Eagleton Stirs Up the Campus with Attack on "Racist" Amis and Son', *Independent*, 4 Oct. 2007.

Carter, Graydon, 'That Summer in Italy', *New York Times*, 21 May 2010.

Cash, William, 'Martian Amis', *Times Saturday Review*, 1 Aug. 1992.
Cowley, Jason, 'Catastrophe Theories', *Observer*, 8 Sept. 2002.
Craig, Amanda, 'Review of *Lionel Asbo*', *Independent*, 10 June 2012.
Diedrick, James, 'From the Ridiculous to the Sublime: The Early Reception of *Night Train*', *Authors Review of Books*, 16 Nov. 1997.
Douglas-Fairhurst, Robert, 'Dickens with a Snarl', *Observer*, 24 Aug. 2003.
Drabble, Margaret, 'Review of *Dead Babies*', *New York Times Book Review*, 8 Feb. 1976.
Dyer, Geoff, 'Down to the Serious Fun of Writing', *Manchester Guardian Weekly*, 14 Nov. 1993.
Ellison, Jane, 'Battle Fields', *Guardian*, 12 Oct. 1989.
Fischer, Tibor, 'Someone Needs to Have a Word with Amis', *Sunday Telegraph*, 4 Aug. 2003.
———, 'It Is Time Martin Amis Wrote a Bona Fide Novel Again', *Sunday Telegraph*, 1 Oct. 2006.
Fremont-Smith, Eliot, 'Review of *The Rachel Papers*', *New York Magazine*, 29 April 1974.
Fuller, Graham, 'Yob Action', *Village Voice*, 1 Dec. 1987.
———, 'Murder He Wrote: Martin Amis's Killing Fields', *Village Voice*, 24 April 1990.
———, 'The Pros and Cons of Martin Amis', *Interview*, 25/5 May 1995.
Gerard, Jasper, 'Is There Still a Masterpiece in the Boy?', *Sunday Times*, 15 April 2001.
Gessen, Keith, 'Growing Up All Wrong', *The Nation*, 8 Dec. 2003.
Getlin, Josh, 'For Martin Amis, It's OK to Lose his Cool', *Los Angeles Times*, 3 Feb. 2007.
Glass, Charles, 'It's Best to Roll with the Big Cats', *Guardian*, 10 Jan. 1995.
Glendenning, Victoria, 'Lamb's Tale from Amis', *Listener*, 5 March 1981.
Goring, Rosemary, 'Still Life in the Old Dog', *Glasgow Herald*, 30 Sept. 2006.
Gross, John, 'Review of *Money*', *New York Times*, 15 March 1985.
Grossman, Lev, 'Q & A with Martin Amis', *Time*, 5 Feb. 2007.
Haffenden, John, 'Martin Amis', *Novelists in Interview* (London and New York: Methuen, 1985), 1–24.
Hamilton, Ian, 'Martin and Martina', *London Review of Books*, 20 Sept. 1984.
Harrison, John M., 'Speeding to Cradle from Grave', *Times Literary Supplement*, 20 Sept. 1991.
Heawood, Jonathan, 'The Books Interview: Martin Amis', *Observer*, 8 Sept. 2002.
Hensher, Philip, 'Nothing Matters More than Prose', *Spectator*, 21 April 2001.

———, 'Treasures Buried in the Mud', *Spectator*, 6 Sept. 2003.
———, 'Review of *The Pregnant Widow*', *Telegraph*, 5 Feb. 2010.
Hitchens, Christopher, 'What Kingsley Really Thought About that "Little Shit" Martin', *Evening Standard*, 8 May 2000.
Hollinghurst, Alan, 'Leader of the Pack', *Guardian*, 6 Sept. 2003.
Hunter-Tilney, Ludovic, 'Gr8 Expectations Even When Off-Form', *Financial Times*, 6 Sept. 2003.
Jones, Lewis, 'The Living V-Sign', *Telegraph*, 26 Jan. 2001.
Jones, Russell Celyn, 'Not Such Light Reading', *Times*, 24 Sept. 1998.
Jordan, Clive, 'Review of *The Rachel Papers*' *Encounter*, Feb. 1974.
Kakutani, Michiko, 'Raging Midlife Crisis as Contemporary Ethos', *New York Times*, 2 May 1995.
———, 'For Writers, Father and Son, Out of Conflict Grew Love', *New York Times*, 23 May 2000.
———, 'Recounting the Suffering of Russia Under Stalin', *New York Times*, 2 May 1995.
———, 'Women May Be from Mars, but Men Are from Hunger', *New York Times*, 28 Oct. 2003.
———, 'Love, Bludgeoned and Bent by the Camps', *New York Times*, 9 Jan. 2007.
———, 'The Sexual Revolution Dissected', *New York Times*, 10 May 2010.
Kaveney, Roz, 'Energy and Entropy", *New Statesman and Society*, 24 March 1995.
Kemp, Peter, 'A Burnt-Out Case' *Sunday Times*, 31 Aug. 2003.
———, 'Review of *The Pregnant Widow*', *Sunday Times*, 31 Jan. 2010.
Kennedy, Douglas, 'Past Troubles Bleed into Present Horrors', *Times*, 30 Sept. 2006.
Kermode, Frank, 'In Reverse', *London Review of Books*, 12 Sept. 1991.
———, 'Nutmegged' , *London Review of Books*, 10 May 2001.
Korn, Eric, 'FrazzledYob-Gene Lag-Jag', *Times Literary Supplement*, 5 Oct. 1984.
Kroll, Jack, 'London Town is Falling Down', *Newsweek*, 5 March 1990.
Lanchester, John, 'As Returning Lord', *London Review of Books*, 7 May 1987.
———, 'Be Interesting', *London Review of Books*, 6 July 2000.
Laurence, Alexander and McGee, Kathleen, 'No More Illusions: Martin Amis Is Getting Old and Wants to Talk About It', *The Write Stuff*, http://www.altx.com/int2/martin.amis.html, (1995), accessed 3 Sept. 2012.
Lawson, Mark, *Front Row*, BBC Radio 4, first broadcast 1 Feb. 2010.
Lee, Hermione, 'Bad Habits in Good Company', *Independent*, 3 Oct. 1993.
Lehman, David, 'From Death to Birth', *New York Times Book Review*, 17

Nov. 1991.

Levin, Bernard, 'Forgetfulness of Things Past', *Sunday Times*, 8 March 1981.

Loose, Julian, 'Satisfaction', *London Review of Books*, 11 May 1995.

Lyall, Sarah, 'For a British Novelist, Tornadoes in August', *New York Times*, 26 Aug. 2003.

McEwan, Ian, 'Interview with Martin Amis', *Guardian Conversations* (London: ICA Video/Trilion, 1988).

McGrath, Patrick, 'Interview with Martin Amis', in Betty Sussler (ed.), *BOMB Interviews* (San Franscisco, Calif.: City Lights Books, 1987), 187–97.

———, 'Her Long Goodbye', *New York Times Book Review*, 1 Feb. 1998.

Malvern, Jack, 'Amis Aims Below the Belt in Attack on Islam', *Times*, 21 Oct. 2002.

Marcus, James, 'History Made Him Do It', *Los Angeles Times*, 14 Jan. 2007.

Mars-Jones, Adam, 'Fireworks at the Funeral', *Times Literary Supplement*, 1 May 1987.

———, 'Looking on the Blight Side', *Times Literary Supplement*, 24 March 1995.

———, 'Books – What Big Boys are Made of', *Observer*, 11 Oct. 1998.

———, 'Anti-Dad', *London Review of Books*, 21 June 2012.

Matthews, David, 'Beyond the Porn, Amis Goes Slack', *Weekend Australian*, 6 Sept. 2003.

Mellors, John, 'Raw Breakfast', *Listener*, 30 Oct. 1976.

Michener, Charles, 'Britain's Brat of Letters', *Esquire*, Jan. 1986.

Miller, Karl, 'A Feast at the Amis Table', *Glasgow Herald*, 25 May 2000.

Moore, Geoffrey, 'Amis Scores a Hit', *Financial Times*, 26 July 2000.

Morrison, Blake, 'Nice and Nasty', *Times Literary Supplement*, 16 Nov. 1973.

Morrison, Susan, 'The Wit and Fury of Martin Amis', *Rolling Stone*, 17 May 1990.

Mount, Harry, 'Review of *The Pregnant Widow*', *Telegraph*, 7 Feb. 2010.

Muir, Kate, 'After His Crucifixion over *Yellow Dog*', *Times Magazine*, 13 Sept. 2003.

Orr, Deborah, 'England is Great', *Independent*, 19 May 2000.

Parini, Jay, 'Men Who Hate Women', *New York Times Book Review*, 6 Sept. 1987.

Pesetsky, Bette, 'Lust Among the Ruins', *New York Times Book Review*, 4 March 1990.

Phillips, Adam, 'Cloud Cover', *London Review of Books*, 16 Oct. 1997.

Power, Carla, 'Growing Up with Kingsley', *Newsweek*, 26 June 2000.

Price, James, 'Review of *Dead Babies*', *Encounter*, Feb. 1976.

Pritchard, William H., 'Getting Old: *The Pregnant Widow*', *Commonweal*,

137/14, 13 Aug. 2010.

Profumo, David, 'Interview: David Profumo Drops in on Martin Amis', *Literary Review*, 107 (1987), 41–2.

Prose, Francine, 'Novelist at Large', *New York Times Book Review*, 27 Feb. 1994.

Pulver, Andrew, 'You Lying Hippies', *Guardian*, 23 Jan. 2001.

Ratcliffe, Michael, 'What Little Boys Are Made Of, *Observer*, 26 March 1995.

Robson, Leo, 'Review of *Lionel Asbo: State of England*', *New Statesman*, 6 June 2012.

———, 'Review of *The Pregnant Widow*', *New Statesman*, 28 Jan. 2010.

Ross, Jean W., 'CA Interview'. *Contemporary Authors, New Revision Series*, 27 (Farmington Mills, Mich.: Thomson Gale, 1989), 23–5.

Scott, A. O., 'Trans-Atlantic Flights', *New York Times Book Review*, 31 Jan. 1999.

Self, Will, 'An Interview with Martin Amis', *Mississippi Review*, 3 Oct. 1993, 143–69.

———, 'Something Amiss in Amis Country', *Esquire*, April 1993.

Service, Robert, 'How Uncle Joe Hoodwinked the West', *Sunday Times*, 25 Aug. 2002.

Sexton, David, 'Marty in His Middle Age', *Guardian*, 28 March 1995.

Shnayerson, Michael, 'Famous Amis', *Vanity Fair*, May 1995.

Shriver, Lionel, 'When Boredom Is a Violent Emotion', *Daily Telegraph*, 7 Oct. 2006.

Silverblatt, Michael, 'Interview with Martin Amis', radio broadcast, *KCRW*, 15 Feb. 2007.

Sissman, L. E., 'Miss, Near Miss, Hit', *New Yorker*, 24 June 1974.

Smith, Aidan, 'Review of *Lionel Asbo: State of England*', *Scotland on Sunday*, 10 June 2012.

Smith, Amanda, 'Martin Amis', *Publishers Weekly*, 8 Feb. 1985.

Soar, Daniel, 'Bile, Blood, Bilge, Mulch', *London Review of Books*, 4 Jan. 2007.

Stead, Deborah, 'The Planet as Murder Victim', *New York Times Book Review*, 4 March 1990.

Stout, Mira, 'Martin Amis: Down London's Mean Streets', *New York Times Book Review*, 4 Feb. 1990.

Summerscale, Kate, 'Martin Amis Leaps Back into the Ring', *Telegraph*, 15 Oct. 2007.

Sutherland, John, 'Dead Babies, Sick Jokes', *Guardian*, 2 May 2001.

Szamuely, George, 'Something Amiss with Martin', *National Review*, 28 May 1990.

Tait, Theo, 'Review of *Lionel Asbo*', *Guardian*, 8 June 2012.

Tandon, Bharat, 'Martin Amis's Chronicle of Loss', *Times Literary Supplement*, 3 Feb. 2010.

Taylor, Christopher, 'Review of *The Pregnant Widow*', *Guardian*, 6 Feb. 2010.

Thubron, Colin, 'Martin Versus Stalin', *Times*, 4 Sept. 2002.

Trueheart, Charles, 'Through a Mirror Darkly', *Washington Post*, 26 Nov. 1991.

Wachtel, Eleanor, 'Eleanor Wachtel with Martin Amis', *Malahat Review*, 114 (1996), 43–58.

Wagner, Erica, 'Tiring Old Tricks', *Times*, 3 Sept. 2003.

Walden, George, 'Back to Blighty', *New Statesman*, 8 Sept. 2003.

Walsh, John, 'Twilight of the Idol? The Knives Are Out for Martin Amis', *Independent*, 27 June 2006.

Walter, Natasha, 'Dark Side of the Tracks', *Guardian Weekly*, 28 Sept. 1997.

Ward, David, 'A Black Comedy of Manners', *Virginia Quarterly Review*, 72/3 (1996), 561–4.

White, Edmund, 'More Lad Than Bad', *New York Review of Books*, 24 June 2010.

Wilson, Jonathan, 'A Very English Story', *New Yorker*, 6 March 1995.

Wood, James, 'Fearful Symmetry of Father and Son', *Guardian*, 20 May 2000.

THEORETICAL TEXTS

Acheson, James and Sarah C. E. Ross (eds), *The Contemporary British Novel since 1980* (Basingstoke and New York: Palgrave, 2005).

Allen, Nicola, *Marginality in the Contemporary British Novel* (London: Continuum, 2008).

Bakhtin, Mikhail, *Problems of Dostoevsky's Poetics*, trans. Caryl Emerson (Minneapolis: University of Minnesota Press, 1984).

Bell, Ian A. (ed.), *Peripheral Visions: Images of Nationhood in Contemporary British Fiction* (Cardiff: University of Wales Press, 1995).

Bentley, Nick (ed.), *British Fiction of the 1990s* (London: Routledge, 2005).

Bickley, Pamela, *Contemporary Fiction: The Novel Since 1990* (Cambridge: Cambridge University Press, 2008).

Bloom, Harold, *The Anxiety of Influence: A Theory of Poetry* (Oxford: Oxford University Press, 1973).

Bradbury, Malcolm, *The Modern British Novel 1878–2001*, 2nd edn (Harmondsworth: Penguin, 2001).

Bradford, Richard, *The Novel Now: Contemporary British Fiction* (Malden, Mass. and Oxford: Blackwell, 2007).

Brannigan, John, *Orwell to the Present: Literature in England, 1945–2000* (Basingstoke and New York: Palgrave, 2003).

Childs, Peter, *Contemporary Novelists: British Fiction Since 1970* (Basingstoke and New York: Palgrave, 2005).

Connor, Steven, *The English Novel in History, 1950–1995* (London: Routledge, 1996).

Currie, Mark, *About Time: Narrative, Fiction and the Philosophy of Time* (Edinburgh: Edinburgh University Press, 2007).

D'Haen, Theo and Hans Bertens (eds), *Postmodern Studies 7: British Postmodern Fiction* (Amsterdam: Rodopi, 1994).

Eliot, George, 'The Natural History of German Life', in *The Essays of George Eliot*, ed. Thomas Pinney (New York: Princeton University Press, 1963), 266–99.

Ferrebe, Alice, *Masculinity in Male-Authored Fiction, 1950–2000: Keeping it Up* (Basingstoke and New York: Palgrave, 2005).

Finney, Brian, *English Fiction Since 1984: Narrating a Nation* (Basingstoke and New York: Palgrave, 2006).

Frye, Northrop, *The Anatomy of Criticism: Four Essays* (Princeton and Oxford: Princeton University Press, [1957] 1971).

Gasiorek, Andrzej, *Post-War British Fiction: Realism and After* (London: Arnold, 1995).

Greaney, Michael, *Contemporary Fiction and the Uses of Theory* (Basingstoke and New York: Palgrave, 2006).

Head, Dominic, *The Cambridge Introduction to Modern British Fiction, 1950–2000* (Cambridge: Cambridge University Press, 2002).

———, *The State of the Novel: Britain and Beyond* (Malden, Mass. and Oxford: Wiley-Blackwell, 2008).

Jameson, Fredric, *Postmodernism, Or the Cultural Logic of Late Capitalism* (London and New York: Verso, 1991).

Lane, Richard J., Rod Mengham and Philip Tew (eds), *Contemporary British Fiction* (Cambridge: Polity, 2003).

Leader, Zachary, *On Modern British Fiction* (Oxford: Oxford University Press, 2002).

Lee, Alison, *Realism and Power: Postmodern British Fiction* (London: Routledge, 1990).

Massie, Alan, *The Novel Today* (London: Longman, 1990).

Mengham, Rod and Philip Tew (eds), *British Fiction Today* (London and New York: Continuum, 2006).

Middleton, Peter and Tim Woods, *Literatures of Memory: History, Time and Space in Postwar Writing* (Manchester: Manchester University Press, 2000).

Morrison, Jago, *Contemporary Fiction* (London: Routledge, 2003).

Palmer, Paulina, *Contemporary Women's Fiction: Narrative Practice and Feminist Theory* (New York: Harvester Wheatsheaf, 1989).

Randall, Martin, *9/11 and the Literature of Terror* (Edinburgh: Edinburgh University Press, 2011).

Rennison, Nick, *Contemporary British Novelists* (London: Routledge,

2004).

Shaffer, Brian W., *Reading the Novel in English 1950–2000* (Malden, Mass. and Oxford: Blackwell, 2006).

Smyth, Edmund (ed.), *Postmodernism and Contemporary Fiction* (London: Batsford, 1991).

Stevenson, Randall, *The Last of England? Vol. 12, The Oxford English Literary History, 1960–2000* (Oxford: Oxford University Press, 2004).

Taylor, D. J., *After the War: The Novel and English Society since 1945* (London: Chatto and Windus, 1993).

Tew, Philip, *The Contemporary British Novel*, 2nd edn (London and New York: Continuum, 2008).

Todd, Richard, *Consuming Fictions: The Booker Prize and Fiction in Britain Today* (London: Bloomsbury, 1996).

Waugh, Patricia, *Harvest of the Sixties: English Literature and its Backgrounds, 1960–1990* (Oxford University Press, 1995).

Worthington, Kim L., *Self as Narrative: Subjectivity and Community in Contemporary Fiction* (Oxford: Oxford University Press, 1996).

Index

Printed and bound by CPI Group (UK) Ltd, Croydon, CR0 4YY

07/07/2026

14916196-0001